ENDING THERAPY

ENDING THERAPY

The Meaning of Termination

Terry A. Kupers, M.D.

NEW YORK UNIVERSITY PRESS
New York and London

Library of Congress Cataloging-in-Publication Data

Kupers, Terry Allen.
   Ending therapy: the meaning of termination/Terry A. Kupers.
      p. cm.
   Bibliography: p.
   Includes index.
   ISBN 0-8147-4594-6 (alk. paper)
   1. Psychotherapy—Termination. I. Title.
RC489.T45K87 1988
616.89′14—dc19   87-35330
                                                              CIP

New York University Press books are Smyth-sewn
and printed on permanent and durable acid-free paper.

Contents

Acknowledgments

MANY OF the ideas presented here I developed while teaching at the Graduate School of Psychology of the Wright Institute, Berkelely. Students there stimulated my thinking about many issues, and I appreciate their input.

The real risk-takers in the therapy venture are the clients. It is only their courage and motivation to change that make the therapist's work possible.

The following people read the manuscript in part or as a whole and made helpful suggestions: Jane Ariel, Gate Battaile, Susan Brown, Richard Lichtman, Lillian Rubin, Arlene Shmaeff, Herb Schreier, and David Socholitzky. Their support and help have been invaluable.

Many thanks to Brian Wilson who, by sitting on the tracks and attempting to halt munitions shipments to Central America, opened our eyes to the real priorities.

Kitty Moore, my editor at New York University Press, has been enthusiastic and encouraging since she first read the manuscript, and her suggestions and editing have been superb.

Special thanks to Arlene Shmaeff for her support, her ideas, and for nurturing the creative spirit in our house.

Introduction

THERE ARE two levels to my discussion of the termination of psychotherapy: the clinical and the social. On the clinical level, there is the issue of what goes on between the therapist and the client. When is the proper time to terminate therapy? How is the termination phase to be conducted so the parting will be constructive and the client will carry on the psychological work after the termination? On the social level, we can explore more general questions regarding the definition of success in therapy. When is the client "cured"? How can we describe the line that separates the part of human unhappiness that we believe to be amenable to therapeutic intervention from the part that we believe is not?

At the end of *Studies on Hysteria* (1895), Freud draws this line between "neurotic misery" and everyday "unhappiness." Freud reports a conversation with an analysand who asked: "Why, you tell me yourself that my illness is probably connected with my circumstances and the events of my life. You cannot alter these in any way. How do you propose to help me, then?" Freud's famous reply: "Much will be gained if we succeed in transforming your hysterical misery into common unhappiness. With a mental life that has been restored to health you will be better armed against that unhappiness" (Freud and Breuer, 1895, p. 305).

As clinicians discover both new intervention techniques and new forms of unhappiness that seem amenable to therapeutic intervention, that line moves, and more of what once might have been considered everyday unhappiness is ceded to the territory of neurotic misery. This progressive psychologization of everyday life directly affects the clinical management of termination in the consulting-room setting and has important social ramifications. A major premise of this book is that the clinical and social issues must be considered together. A discussion that is limited to the clinical issues misses much of the meaning of termination and, as I will show in chapter 7, is ultimately unable to address those clinical questions adequately.

Though this is mainly a discussion of psychotherapy, and not psychoanalysis, I will begin in chapter 1 with Freud's thoughts about termination. The modern therapist is heir to Freud's body of work, even without an explicit theoretical link, if only because of the place Freud won for the talking cure in our lives. Beginning with Freud's work also provides a common starting point for clinicians of varying theoretical persuasions and offers a well-defined set of terms.

The discussion will move on to later developments in the field of psychoanalysis (chapter 2) and psychotherapy (chapter 3). Of course, with the newer developments, one finds more diversity among clinicians, and fewer shared assumptions. There is no founder or single monolithic institute to foster orthodoxy and uniformity of thought. The further the discussion moves from Freud's original formulations, the more I will need to define terms and illustrate points with my own clinical material.

Chapter 3 explores the concrete clinical issues. When is the proper time to terminate therapy? The therapist's task is to find a point somewhere in between a premature termination, where the results of the therapy quickly unravel, and an excessively long and dependent therapeutic relationship. The clinician must then help the client prepare to say goodbye and to carry on the psychological work on his or her own. The client's concern is generally about what will happen after therapy ends. "Will I lose the strength I feel being in therapy with you?" Ann asks anxiously. Roger admits that the difficulty he had trusting me at the beginning of therapy had to do with "exactly what is happening right now—just when you've become an important part of my life, you're saying it's time to stop and say goodbye."

In chapter 4 I will explain the clinical logic that guides the practitioner in deciding, for example, how much therapy is indicated in a given case. The rule of thumb is that the more severe the psychopathology, the longer-lasting the symptoms, and the more pervasive the dysfunction, the longer the therapy required to effect a cure. As more symptoms are considered amenable to therapeutic intervention, new theories evolve to explain the etiology of the symptoms, and new therapeutic techniques proliferate. One result is the trend for therapies to lengthen, to probe more deeply, with the aim of altering more profound underlying structures of the psyche. Another trend, following the same logic, is to employ brief therapy when the symptoms are circumscribed or short-lived and when the client seems capable of rapid change.

In chapter 4 I use Heinz Kohut's self psychology to illustrate the clinical logic that I believe underlies most post-Freudian developments in the field. This does not mean I believe that Kohut's is the single most important contribution. Nor is it the only one I could use to illustrate the logic. I will show how each new development—including the character analysis of Wilhelm Reich, Melanie Klein's work, the object-relations theory of W. R. D. Fairbairn, Kohut's self psychology, and even the turn toward brief therapy—follows a recognizable logical progression, and how that logic leads to further encroachment of the realm of psychopathology onto the territory that once might have been considered part of our common unhappiness.

Chapter 5 discusses brief psychotherapy. There are two basic ways to decide when to terminate a therapy. Either the termination can be left open-ended, in which case it is possible to give the client much of the responsibility for deciding when to end the therapy, or a date can be chosen in advance, even at the commencement, and throughout the process the participants know how much time remains. The brief therapists use the latter technique. The client in brief therapy may experience strong feelings about the therapist's dictating the terms, and perhaps will feel that she or he is being shortchanged in the process. Thus the framework of brief therapy highlights some important termination issues.

The practice of brief therapy, or better, the social distribution of the modality, also brings out a contradiction in the clinical logic, which is presented in chapter 4. If clients who fit the selection criteria for brief or long-term psychotherapy, be they rich or poor, were offered quality therapy of the kind indicated for their condition, then the clinical logic would hold true. But this is not at all the case. A patient's financial means usually play a greater part in determining the length of therapy than does clinical condition. Those who can afford only brief therapy—and I include here those whose insurance or health plan covers only a limited number of sessions—will have little choice in the matter. Meanwhile, therapists are more likely to tell those who have more health coverage or can afford to pay private fees that their condition warrants long-term therapy. If we limited our discussion only to the clinical issues regarding the length of therapy, we would miss entirely this important social dynamic.

In chapter 6 I address what might seem to be a contradiction in my argument: I first claim that psychoanalyses and therapies have tended to lengthen and then state that there has been a countertendency toward brief therapy (chapter 5). Is this not a contradiction? Actually, the length of any particular therapy is not at issue. In chapter 6 I argue that it is the lifetime total accrued hours in therapy that matter. In other words, an individual consumer of therapy is likely to enter therapy several times. One or more of the therapies will likely be long-term, and several others brief. Each time, the client will think in terms of accomplishing a "piece of work," always with the option of returning to the present therapist, or perhaps another, to do another piece of work when another crisis occurs. The same psychologization that causes long-term therapies to lengthen also causes the total number of hours spent in therapy to increase. In this context, brief therapy can be seen as another way in which people spend more time in therapy. It is also a very useful way for those who repeatedly reenter therapy to do a series of pieces of work.

Chapter 7 focuses on the social level and concentrates on the effect of certain social events on the clinical situation. Perhaps Freud drew that line between neurotic misery and everyday unhappiness because he feared that an army of therapists, knowledgeable in his theories, would one day overrun the turf of what he called everyday unhappiness and claim it for psychopathology. He may have wanted to distinguish between what he felt therapy might alter and what was properly beyond its scope.

Therapists today continue to expand their theories and create therapeutic strategies in order to conquer more and more aspects of everyday unhappiness. The trend in the field is toward the diagnosis of ever more varied psychopathologies to justify ever more psychotherapy for just about anyone. The literature is filled with descriptions of the new diagnostic categories—from narcissistic personalities and posttraumatic stress disorders to mid-life crises and impostor syndromes in high achieving women—and results of research about the efficacy of treatment techniques.

There is a growing community of psychologically sophisticated people, whom I term "therapy consumers," who have an abstract commitment to therapy. They believe in therapy and feel they will grow from the experience. In times of crisis, they consult a therapist. And, of course, the conditions to be diagnosed and the issues to be addressed in therapy expand to fit the modern client's willingness to endure more therapy and ability to pay the fees. The community of therapy consumers provides the best customers: sane, relatively successful, but unhappy clients who visit therapists of their own accord. These are the clients who most often frequent private consulting rooms.

Some complain of depression, or a feeling of inner emptiness, panic attacks, or marital tensions; some complain of a crisis in the family; still others talk of a lack of success or fulfillment at work. Some want a short course of therapy to help alleviate certain symptoms. Others seek a long-term, open-ended therapy in which they can get to know themselves better and make some serious changes in their lives. These people often believe that they are entitled to happiness and that some inner flaw causes their unhappiness. Because happiness seems so elusive and because of their strong commitment to therapy, they are willing to spend endless hours in therapists' consulting rooms. The issue of termination for these clients is very different than it is for others. For more severely disturbed and dysfunctional clients, for instance, therapy is not such an elective matter, and the decision about when to terminate is more dependent on the client's level of stability. These clients are not the focus here; I have discussed their therapy and its termination elsewhere (Kupers, 1981). Chapter 7 focuses on the way the evolution of a community of therapy consumers affects the termination of therapy.

In the Conclusion I return to a theme Freud discussed in "Analysis Terminable and Interminable" (1937). The modern therapist, constantly in search of the cure for previously untreatable human foibles, has long ago lost sight of the line between psychopathology and everyday unhappiness. Therapy, which can be defined as either one long-term relationship or a series of different therapeutic encounters, becomes interminable. As this subject cannot be approached solely from a narrow clinical focus, it is not surprising that it is entirely absent from the clinical literature. But social dynamics—for instance, the inequitable distribution of different lengths of treatment or the tendency for the community of therapy consumers to undergo longer and repeated psychotherapies—play a large part in determining when and how termination is managed in the consulting room, whether or not the clinician is aware of the interplay of the clinical and social levels.

Chapter 1

Freud on Termination

FREUD ENJOYED telling the story of the "free house," the point in a town where no arrests would be made, no matter what the crimes of people assembled there. "How long would it be before all the riff-raff of the town had collected there?" (Freud, 1913, p. 136). The same would be true of the psyche if we (analyst and analysand) left a stone unturned in our quest for the unconscious truth. All the shadowy aspects of unconscious life would gravitate there and remain resistant to analysis, inaccessible to conscious expression. Here is the reason for the basic rule of psychoanalysis: tell all that comes to mind, even the trivial and the embarrassing.

The termination of psychoanalysis can easily become a psychological free house, if only because the two parties have no opportunity afterward to meet and examine together the leftover issues and feelings between them. Thus there is a need for a "termination phase" to the analysis, a period before the last session during which the analyst must dig deeply to locate, and help the analysand work through, the analysand's feelings and fantasies about the termination. Otherwise, those untouched concerns, like the issues that congregate in a free house, will be acted out later and will subvert the potential for a successful cure.

Freud did not arrive at this formulation about termination until very late in his career. Initially, he and his inner circle had not viewed termination as an important event at all. In his early cases, ignoring of termination issues caused serious clinical failures. I will briefly discuss three of those early cases, two of which must be counted as totally failed terminations (Anna O. and Dora) and the third as a bracketed termination (the Wolfman), since the analysand continued to be attached to Freud and to the psychoanalytic movement for the remainder of his life.

Anna O.

During Freud's early collaboration with Josef Breuer, when hypnosis and catharsis played key roles in the evolving practice of psychoanalysis, they experienced a dramatic failed termination that neither made mention of in their published reports of the case (Freud and Breuer, 1895; Freud, 1910). The now famous case of Anna O. (Bertha Pappenheim, 1859-1936), was actually Breuer's case. Anna O. was twenty-one when she went to see Breuer for a nervous cough. Her symptoms also included hysterical paralysis of one side of her body with contractures and anesthesia, transient disturbances of speech and sight, somnambulism and afternoon states of somnolence, "absences," hallucinations, and a remarkable tendency for symptoms to be ameliorated after she had an opportunity to narrate her experience. She seemed a perfect candidate for Breuer's hypnosis-and-talking treatment of hysteria, and he saw her almost daily for eighteen months. Under hypnosis she talked, and the result was a striking improvement in her symptomatology.

The apparent problem in this case was Breuer's countertransference. According to Ernest Jones (1953, 1:223-25), Breuer was so absorbed in the case that he talked about Anna O. incessantly, even with his wife. His wife became bored, then jealous, and, seemingly unable to express either sentiment, she became depressed. When Breuer eventually noticed his wife's reaction, he decided to terminate the treatment of Anna O. immediately. Anna O. seemed to take the news well, and said goodbye. Later that evening, Breuer was called back to see her because she had suffered a relapse. All her symptoms had returned, and she appeared to be in the throes of a hysterical childbirth (pseudocyesis). Breuer, who had obviously been denying the romantic implications of their therapeutic relationship, was shocked. He proceeded to calm her by hypnotizing her and then fled from the house. The next day he and his wife left on a second honeymoon.

The termination was a fiasco. There was no preparation for the parting, no resolution of the transference, and not even any understanding of what had gone wrong. Anna O. then deteriorated further and was admitted to a mental institution. Eventually she recovered enough to become the first social worker in Germany, though she never married and led a somewhat constricted life.

This dramatically failed analysis and termination reflect the small place given to analysis of the transference in those early days of psychoanalysis. Freud and Breuer considered the transference an unfortunate complication of the treatment, something to be avoided if at all possible so the analysis would not be derailed, as it was in the case of Anna O. Freud later wrote to his fiancée about the case, and when she expressed fear that the same kind of romantic entanglement might develop between him and his female analysands, he rejoined with false modesty: "For that to happen one has to be a Breuer" (letter to Martha Bernays, Nov. 11, 1883, cited in Jones, 1953, 1:225). In fact, Freud would later find transference to be omnipresent and, instead of viewing it as extrinsic to the proper work of analysis, would begin to see the analysis of the transference as the central task and mutative factor in the progress of the cure. Even so, Freud's (1937) formulation about termination, though brilliant on the issues he attends to, ignores important aspects of the termination process— for instance, the real loss the two participants experience, and the countertransference. I will discuss these issues after presenting two more of his cases.

Dora

Freud's analysis of Dora was a turning point in his views on the transference. Once again, it was a failed termination—Dora abruptly and unilaterally broke off the analysis—that would focus his attention on the transference.

Dora, eighteen, was sent to Freud by her father, who had been Freud's patient years earlier. She suffered spells of difficulty in breathing (dyspnea) from age eight and had visited Freud once before at age sixteen because of a cough and hoarseness— symptoms that Freud deemed hysterical. When these symptoms continued, Dora's father sent her to Freud a second time. In addition, he was concerned that Dora had grown irritable and distant from him and he had been convinced by a close friend, Herr K., that she had a too lively sexual imagination.

Dora was very attached to her father, with whom she shared a lively intellectual exchange. He was often ill, had been treated by Freud for symptoms of syphilis, and later developed tuberculosis. Freud described Dora's mother as suffering from a "housewife's psychosis." Freud quickly learned that the family's romantic life was quite complicated. Because of the father's illness, the family had moved from Vienna to a small town and had become quite close to another family, the K.'s. Dora babysat for the K. children. Frau K., a vivacious woman, became friend, then nurse, and finally lover to Dora's father. During this period, Herr K. began to make advances toward Dora.

When Dora was fourteen and visiting Herr K.'s office, he evidently kissed her passionately on the mouth. When she was sixteen, she told her mother he had propositioned her. Herr K., who had until then spent a great deal of time with Dora and bestowed various gifts upon her, began to convince her parents that she thought about sex too much and that any improprieties were purely figments of her overactive imagination. Dora asked her father to break off the family's relationship with the K.'s. Perhaps because he believed Herr K. and not his own daughter, but more likely because he did not want to end his affair with Frau K., he refused. She became angry and aloof. She fell into a depression, her cough worsened, and she isolated herself, particularly from males. Her father became convinced all this arose from her illness, and he brought her to Freud.

Freud's written report focuses on two of Dora's dreams. His interpretations, and his method in arriving at them, are a continuation of his then recently published *The Interpretation of Dreams* (Freud, 1900). He uses Dora's case material to continue his polemical argument that the repressed sexual life of children—real or imagined—is at the core of hysteria and the other neuroses.

Interestingly, in his discussion he gives us a glimpse of his analytic technique at the time. Still very much the detective looking for unconscious sexual memories and fantasies, he sought at one point to link Dora's hysterical cough with her fantasies of oral sex. In order to prove to her that this was the case, he confronted her with a contradiction in her logic:

> I pointed out the contradiction she was involved in if on the one hand she continued to insist that her father's relation with Frau K. was a common love-affair, and on the other hand maintained that her father was impotent, or in other words incapable of carrying on an affair of such a kind. Her answer showed that she had no need to admit the contradiction. She knew very well, she said, that there was more than one way of obtaining sexual gratification. . . . I could then go on to say that in that case she must be thinking of precisely those parts of the body which in her case were in a state of irrita-tion—the throat and the oral cavity. (Freud, 1905a, p. 47)

Dora denied this interpretation. But Freud persisted until, "A very short time after she had tacitly accepted this explanation her cough vanished." Freud's frontal assault on Dora's resis-tances, and his conviction that insight into previously repressed ideas would alleviate the symptoms, are repeatedly demon-strated in this case. Many brief therapists of today borrow and even enlarge on the confrontational, insight-oriented style Freud used during this period (Davanloo, 1978).

Just when Freud felt progress was being made in the analysis, Dora decided to terminate. The following exchange occurred:

> She opened the third sitting with these words: "Do you know that I am here for the last time today?"
>
> "How can I know, as you have said nothing to me about it?"
>
> "Yes, I made up my mind to put up with it till the New Year. But I shall wait no longer than that to be cured."
>
> "You know that you are free to stop the treatment at any time. But for today we will go on with our work." (Freud, 1905a, p. 105)

Freud continued to analyze the contents of Dora's associations during that session, and when the hour was over they said good-bye. In a postscript to the case, Freud wonders whether the analysis would not have continued longer if he had been more insistent and more openly warm and interested in continuing to see her. He goes on to a discussion of the transference, which by this time he sees as a critical part of the analytic encounter. He writes: "Nevertheless, transference cannot be evaded, since use is made of it in setting up all the obstacles that make the material inaccessible to treatment, and since it is only after the transference has been resolved that a patient arrives at a sense of conviction of the validity of the connections which have been constructed during the analysis" (Freud, 1905a, pp. 116-17). Finally, he criticizes his management of Dora's case: "I have been obliged to speak of transference, for it is only by means of this factor that I can elucidate the peculiarities of Dora's analysis. Its great merit, namely, the unusual clarity which makes it seem so suitable as a first introductory publication, is closely bound up with its great defect, which led to its being broken off prematurely. I did not succeed in mastering the transference in good time" (Freud, 1905a, p. 118). It has been suggested that Freud was also not in touch with the countertransference and that he had some romantic interest in Dora (Gill and Muslin, 1978). Still, it is to his credit that in reviewing a failed case, Freud makes the link between termination and resolution of the transference that would dominate all future psychoanalytic and psychotherapeutic discussions about termination.

But Dora's relationship with Freud was not entirely one of transference. Among others, Maria Ramas (1980), in a feminist critique of the case, and Richard Lichtman (1982), in a Marxist rereading of Freud's clinical discussion, stress what Freud knew (though he made little of this knowledge) of the family history and the cultural context of the time: namely, that Dora was passed from her father to Herr K., and then to Freud, almost as barter. The father forced Herr K.'s presence on Dora so that the father could have an affair with Frau K., and then, in order to avoid having to end the affair, when Dora became upset he passed her on to Freud. Thus Lichtman notes Freud's statement that Dora's father "handed her over to me for psychotherapeutic treatment." According to Lichtman,

The phrase is not an accident. Instead, it points to the fact that an identical structure lies behind the initiation of Dora's therapy by her father and his tacit bribe of Herr K. through the "gift" of his daughter. Dora's father wanted simply to be let alone and he contrived to accomplish this task by bartering his daughter to Herr K. on the one hand, and by seeking Freud's assistance in making Dora herself more compliant, on the other. . . . The exchange of women for the sake of continued masculine domination, either as price affixed to a commodity or in the form of barter as an equivalent of "items of exchange," is almost too obvious to ignore. (Lichtman, 1982, p. 142)

Ramas situates the social reality of the barter of women in the context of the domination and debasement middle-class women generally suffered in heterosexual relationships in turn-of-the-century Austria. For instance, she mentions that Dora's father was infected with venereal diseases while living a loose life and then gave those diseases to Dora's mother, who subsequently suffered from the physical symptoms. Freud overlooked this bit of reality when he diagnosed her "housewife's psychosis." According to Ramas, the woman's role was to be submissive and to be debased in the heterosexual act—and then to enjoy it, or to pretend to—so Dora's hysteria might be interpreted as a righteous protest against "patriarchal sexuality, and a protest against postoedipal femininity" (p. 478).

These views are quite in contrast to Freud's. Freud felt it was a sign of Dora's neurosis that she was not excited by Herr K.'s advances. Thus Lichtman and Ramas are both suggesting that it was Freud's actual collusion with her father and Herr K. in their debasement of women that Dora was protesting by fleeing from the analysis, and not a transference distortion on Dora's part. Since Freud did not give any credence to the actual relationships that Dora perceptively understood, she could not discuss her plight with Freud, and therefore Freud did not have enough credibility for her to risk staying in treatment and making herself vulnerable by discussing sexual secrets. Whether one wishes to consider the issue on a strictly transference-countertransference level, or to consider the plight of women in that social context, it is clear that the premature termination resulted directly from Freud's biases and mistakes.

The Wolfman

The case of the Wolfman is remarkable in several regards. First, Freud experimented with a novel approach to termination in that he set the date of the final session a year in advance. Second, in his written discussion of the case, Freud ignored the material that today would be the focus of the termination phase of a psychoanalysis or psychotherapy. And finally, in spite of the time-limit innovation, the Wolfman's analysis was essentially interminable, for he became a lifetime analysand and what we might call an "honorary member" of the psychoanalytic community.

The Wolfman, a twenty-four-year-old Russian, the son of a lawyer and big landowner in Odessa, was so disabled by various emotional symptoms that he was unable to work for most of his adult life. He first visited Freud in Vienna in 1910. He underwent psychoanalysis with Freud for four and a half years, and then again for several months in 1919, after his family had lost its land and fortune and he had to leave revolutionary Russia (Freud, 1918). Later he underwent analysis twice more with Freud's student, Ruth Mack Brunswick, whom he saw for several months in 1926-27; after a two-year hiatus he saw her again irregularly for several more years; and finally, after his wife's suicide, he saw her for six more weeks in 1938 (Mack Brunswick, 1928). Then, through occasional visits and sporadic correspondence, he maintained a quasi-analytic relationship with the third major analyst in his life, Muriel Gardiner. Gardiner has collected some of the Wolfman's autobiographical writings, Freud's and Mack Brunswick's case reports, and some of her own impressions and correspondence in a book that gives a multidimensional perspective on this interesting case of Freud's (Wolfman, 1971).

The Wolfman (initials S. P., name withheld by Freud in the interest of anonymity) had a sister, older by two years, who was much favored by their father because of her superior intelligence and probably because of a triangle within the family. His mother, plagued by various physical and psychosomatic ailments, was basically inattentive to the boy's needs—unless he was ill, in which case she would revert to being nurse and caretaker until he was well enough for her to turn her attention elsewhere. The family owned two large estates near Odessa, living at one during the winters and at the other summers. He and his sister were raised by a series of servants, tutors, and caretakers, while his parents, rich enough to be idle much of the time, engaged in a busy social life and traveled often, leaving the children with the caretakers. One caretaker, Nanya, a nurse, was with the Wolfman for many years and played an important part in his development.

The Wolfman early embarked on a career as a lawyer. His emotional crises seemed to overwhelm his capacity to study, so that he did poorly in law school and dropped out. His physical and mental condition had been deteriorating ever since he acquired gonorrhea at age seventeen or eighteen. He then entered a series of sanitariums around Europe, even visiting the famous Emil Kraepelin for a consultation on his condition. In fact, Kraepelin felt he was severely disturbed and sent him to one of the sanitariums. There he met a caretaker-nurse, Therese, who would become his wife. His sister, who had a brilliant early school career, apparently became increasingly depressed and confused. When the Wolfman was nineteen, she committed suicide. After that his father turned more attention toward the Wolfman. In 1908 his father died, also of suicide (there was a long history of psychosis and depression in the family). The Wolfman's various mental symptoms subsequently worsened. He wandered from doctor to doctor and from sanitarium to sanitarium until he came under the care of Dr. D., one of the few Russian practitioners of Freud's psychoanalysis. Dr. D. felt that the Wolfman was a suitable candidate for psychoanalysis but that he did not have sufficient expertise to conduct the cure. So he accompanied his patient to Vienna, where began the Wolfman's first encounter with Freud.

At the time Freud wrote his report of the case, he was in the thick of his argument with Jung and Adler, among others, about the centrality of childhood sexuality in the etiology of the neuroses. To argue his case best, he opted to write about the Wolfman's childhood neurosis, the one involving a wolf phobia and some obsessional symptoms, and less about the neurosis and symptoms of his adult life—even though it was the latter that brought the Wolfman to Freud. The essay demonstrates Freud's logic and detective work in arriving at an interpretation of a dream about wolves that the Wolfman had at age five. Only by reading Ernest Jones's biography of Freud does one learn that the Wolfman "initiated the first hour of treatment with the offer to have rectal intercourse with Freud and then to defecate on his head!" (Jones, 1955, 2:274). Freud's case report makes hardly any comment about the transference, and only by reading Mack Brunswick's later addendum to the case does one learn just how intense the transference was with Freud. And, except for mentioning that he did first attempt the setting of a time limit on the end of the analysis in this case, Freud says nothing about termination. Thus the case report is a brilliant illustration of the unraveling of dreams and neurotic symptoms in the quest for unconscious truths, but it tells us little about the practice of therapy or its termination. But we have other sources for the latter.

Freud learned from the Wolfman that his sister had experimented sexually with him when he was about four. She had played with his genitals. He felt passive in the event, and somewhat humiliated. Beginning with this revelation, the Wolfman eventually revealed a dream he had about wolves soon after this incident with his sister. In the dream, a group of white wolves were sitting on a tree just across from the dreamer's open window. Freud culled from the dream and the Wolfman's associations to it these ideas: "A real occurrence—dating from a very early period—looking—immobility—sexual problems—castration—his father—something terrible" (Wolfman, 1971, p. 179). Freud and the Wolfman eventually arrived at the interpretation that the latter had witnessed his parents having intercourse when he was a year and a half old. The intercourse was from behind (*a tergo*), as the wolves do it. The Wolfman probably identified with his mother—that is, wanted to be "taken" by his father from the rear. Remember, he would be passive in the later sexual episode with his sister, and it would always be his father's love he would crave.

These facets of the case provided Freud an opportunity to discuss his theory of bisexuality. Because of the angle from which the Wolfman witnessed the primal scene, he could see that his mother had no external genital organ. Sometime later he must

have figured that, if he were to be father's receptive sexual partner, he would have to be castrated. Here was Freud's interpretation of the Wolfman's dream and his symptoms. Thus his later
obsessional symptoms—such as his rigid religious beliefs, which
caused him to go through a long ritual of kissing a number of
religious objects before retiring each night—were attempts to
repress this childhood sexual drama and the bisexuality and masochistic strivings that accompanied the unconscious fantasies.

In this case report, another side of Freud emerges. Besides
the battering down of resistances that he practiced in the case
of Dora, Freud could be gentle and tentative in his interpretations—or, as Winnicott would later formulate it (1971b), he
could wait for the analysand to arrive at his own interpretations.
Thus, towards the end of the analysis, the Wolfman associated
to a butterfly with yellow stripes that had frightened him as a
young child (during one stage of childhood he also tortured in-
sects and small animals). Freud guessed incorrectly:

> I will not conceal the fact that at the time I put forward the
> possibility that the yellow stripes on the butterfly had re-
> minded him of similar stripes upon a piece of clothing worn
> by some women. I only mention this as an illustration to show
> how inadequate the physician's constructive efforts usually are
> for clearing up questions that arise, and how unjust it is to
> attribute the results of analysis to the physician's imagination
> and suggestion. (Freud, 1918, p. 89)

Months later, his analysand supplied the missing link: the butterfly's wings reminded him of a woman opening her legs. Freud
comments: "This was an association which I could never have
arrived at myself, and which gained importance from a consideration of the thoroughly infantile nature of the train of associations which it revealed" (Freud, 1918, p. 90).

Once again Freud provides a thrilling, detectivelike search for
the unconscious themes that, when brought to the surface, might
cure the neurosis. But he says little about the actual results, or
even about the actual therapy that occurred. About these we
learn more from the Wolfman himself and from Mack Brunswick's
later report. The Wolfman reports about his infatuation with Freud
and his ideas, about how good he felt that the great master con-

sidered him an interesting intellectual and an interesting case, and about the events of his life such as the ups and downs he experienced with his wife.

The Wolfman provides us with an account of how Freud handled their termination:

> In the weeks before the end of my analysis, we often spoke of the danger of the patient's feeling too close a tie to the therapist. If the patient remains "stuck" in the transference, the success of the treatment is not a lasting one, as it soon becomes evident that the original neurosis has been replaced by another. In this connection, Freud was of the opinion that at the end of treatment a gift from the patient could contribute, as a symbolic act, to lessening his feeling of gratitude and his consequent dependence on the physician. So we agreed that I would give Freud something as a remembrance. As I knew of his love for archeology, the gift I chose for him was a female Egyptian figure, with a miter-shaped headdress. Freud placed it on his desk. (Wolfman, 1971, p. 150)

Thus Freud was much more cognizant of the importance of termination than one might guess from the absence of comment about it in this and other case reports, and he had even created a ritual to mark it. Still, as later reports of the case would demonstrate, the transference and the termination were not sufficiently worked through to permit a totally successful outcome of the analysis.

After his original analysis with Freud, the Wolfman returned to Russia, and functioned significantly better. The Russian Revolution resulted in his family's losing its holdings, and the Wolfman migrated back to Vienna in 1919. At that time, he suffered from some symptoms of the bowel and returned to Freud for a brief second analysis. Freud treated him for free and collected money to provide him with financial support for the next six years. Freud explained this kindness as a return for all the Wolfman had done for psychoanalysis by being a famous case. Was Freud here acting out an unresolved countertransference conflict? In any case, the Wolfman's bowel symptoms cleared up, and he was able to find a job with an insurance company, which he would keep until he retired in 1950.

The Wolfman remained relatively symptom-free until 1926, at which time Freud arranged for him to undergo another psycho-analysis with Ruth Mack Brunswick. When he went to see her, he was suffering from an *idée fixe*, an obsessional fixation on a wound or slight deformity on his nose. According to her account, he wove a complicated paranoid delusional system around the nose deformity, including the notion that a doctor who had treated him for it was trying to harm him and that he would have to murder the doctor. According to Mack Brunswick's interpretation, the nose, being the only other midline protu-berance on the human body, represented the penis, and the Wolfman's obsession and paranoid ideas represented massive castration anxiety. Further, the Wolfman displaced feelings he had about Freud onto the doctor who treated his nose condition. From Mack Brunswick's account we learn that a strong trans-ference with Freud remained unresolved. He alternately praised Freud as the great master and resolved he would have to kill the man who had let him down in important ways. Mack Brunswick's masterful analysis of the transference resulted in an impressive alleviation of the paranoid symptomatology.

As one reads the history of this case and reports by Freud and Mack Brunswick of the analyses, a pattern emerges in the Wolfman's handling of the many losses he endured. At an early age, his parents left him and his sister with caretakers while they took trips and vacations. His mother was often sick and inattentive. His father went to a sanitarium because of severe depression when the Wolfman was five. Then his sister died when he was nineteen, and his father when he was twenty-one, both by suicide. Other family members died. He lost his fortune and had to leave his estates and his native Russia after the Russian Revolution. The analysts to whom he felt close left Vienna when Hitler took control. And finally, his wife committed suicide in 1938. The pattern was that the Wolfman, in very narcissistic fashion, was unable to mourn fully. Instead, he would with each new tragedy attach his emotional energy to a new object, and as he felt inspired by the new person in his life, or hopeful that the new relationship would bring solutions to his unremitting problems, his depression would lift. Thus, when his sister died, he failed to mourn, but rather decided to take flowers to the grave of a favorite poet. When the decision was made that he would travel to Europe and see a doctor who might help his condition, the prospect of this new therapeutic relationship helped to alleviate his depression and other symptoms. When his father died, he turned to Freud: "My father had died only a short time before, and Professor Freud's outstanding personality was able to fill this void" (Wolfman, 1971, p. 89). And when he lost touch with Ruth Mack Brunswick, he quickly turned his attention to Muriel Gardiner, his new friend and analyst. This pattern, when noticed by the astute clinician, would indicate that the termination of an analysis would be problematic, and the liklihood would be great that the client would seek to form a chronic dependency relationship. But these are issues that Freud ignored, likely because of countertransference and his inability to look at dependency, his own as well as his analysand's.

After World War II, and after the analysts who had fled from Nazi-occupied lands were somewhat established in America, England, and Western Europe, Muriel Gardiner, a young medical student at the time she met the Wolfman in prewar Vienna, began corresponding with him and bringing news of recent developments in his life to the psychoanalytic community. In the volume she edited, she includes letters, essays she wrote about the Wolfman, and essays that the Wolfman wrote and that she read for him at meetings of analysts in the United States. She even arranged to sell his paintings at analytic meetings and send him the money. In other words, the Wolfman had by the 1950s become a celebrity in the analytic community. He would never really leave Freud, since he would be part of Freud's family. The great man's wisdom would always be available through the kind attention of another generation of analysts, who were, from their side, very interested in staying in touch with their founder, even if that meant knowing about the later developments of a famous case.

The Wolfman would report that Freud considered him "a piece of psychoanalysis" (Wolfman, 1971, p. 150). There was some kind of collusion with Freud in the Wolfman's dependency, first on Freud and later on psychoanalysis as an institution. Freud seemed to ignore, perhaps even deny, this aspect of the case. We know from Freud's decision to treat the Wolfman gratis in 1919 and to set up a fund for him that a successful outcome in this case mattered a great deal to Freud. And we know from Mack Brunswick's account that Freud never completely worked through the negative transference before terminating. The Wolfman maintained a homicidal rage toward Freud, perhaps because of Freud's deserting him.

The Wolfman became hooked for life on psychoanalysis, as many others would later be. As I will show in chapter 7, psychotherapy eventually supplanted psychoanalysis among a large community of consumers, and the kind of enthusiasm for psychodynamic insight, and the psychoanalytic camp, that the Wolfman demonstrated in his writings would be carried on in its more popular version as a tendency to undergo psychotherapy repeatedly and to maintain a fascination with pop psychology and lay analyzing.

From his published case reports and what we know of these cases through other published accounts, we see that Freud did not pay much attention to termination issues early in his career as an analyst. Later, he began to formulate some ideas on the subject but generally did not consider them critical to the analysis, and hence he did not give sufficient time and energy to working through termination issues. With the Wolfman, his suggestion that his analysand avoid excessive dependency and give him a gift on parting shows that Freud was undoubtedly aware of the danger of unresolved transference and un-worked-through termination, but the results demonstrate that Freud did not give enough time or serious attention to these issues in practice.

"Psychoanalysis Terminable and Interminable"

Freud wrote little more about the termination of analysis until his 1937 essay. Because this essay is his most extensive public discussion of the subject, I am going to explore some of the salient points here. He begins with a polemic against attempts by other analysts, notably Otto Rank, with whom he had had a falling out, to shorten psychoanalysis. Noting that such attempts to accomplish more in a shorter time, or to "accelerate the tempo of analytic therapy," might fit conveniently into "the rush of American life," he cautions that it would accomplish no more "than if the fire-brigade, called to deal with a house that had been set on fire by an overturned oil-lamp, contented themselves with removing the lamp from the room in which the blaze had started" (Freud, 1937, pp. 216-17).

After this beginning, Freud explains his strategy for terminating therapy with the Wolfman. According to him, the reasons were as follows: The analysis had gone on for several years, and while some symptoms were gone and some remained, the process seemed mired. Freud perhaps had an inkling that the Wolfman enjoyed being in analysis with him too much—that is, the analysis was too gratifying—so he told his analysand that the analysis would end a year hence. According to Freud, his strategy worked. Some of the resistances fell away, and the last year of the analysis was more productive than any of the prior three.

Freud then asks the crucial question: "Is there such a thing as a natural end to an analysis—is there any possibility at all of bringing an analysis to such an end?" (Freud 1937, p. 219). His answer provides the framework for much of the subsequent debate. He answers that an analysis is not properly ended until three requirements are met: First, the patient is no longer suffering from former symptoms. Second, there is an indication that these symptoms will not reappear. As he states, "The analyst shall judge that so much repressed material has been made conscious, so much that was unintelligible has been explained, and so much internal resistance conquered, that there is not need to fear a repetition of the pathological processes concerned" (p. 219). And third, the patient is not likely to experience any further significant change by continuing the analysis. As Freud states, "What we are asking is whether the analyst has had such a farreaching influence on the patient that no further change could be expected to take place in him if his analysis were continued" (p. 219).

This is such a lucid conceptualization of what termination is about that, in my opinion, it has never been supplanted in the literature of psychoanalysis and psychotherapy. It has been fleshed out with a long list of details the clinician might watch for to know when the criteria have been satisfied. In addition, the various points have been debated. For instance, some brief therapists now argue that symptom reduction is a sufficient therapeutic goal, although they differentiate the aims of brief therapy from those of analysis, and when they practice psychoanalysis, they are more likely to approximate the criteria Freud carved out (Davanloo, 1978; Sifneos, 1972).

For Freud, as for many clinicians today, symptom reduction is necessary but not sufficient. Enough analytic work must be completed to insure against the return of the symptoms. For instance, if clinicians merely watch for the disappearance of symptoms, how are they to know when only a "transference cure" has been effected, a temporary resolution of symptoms caused by the therapist's actual presence in the client's life? Freud (1914) in fact believed that the symptoms should resolve soon after commencement of the analysis, because the conflictual energy is displaced into a "transference neurosis" that evolves in the consulting room and is accessible to analytic working through (Laplanche and Pontalis, 1973, p. 463). In this short essay on termination, Freud makes little mention of the resolution of the transference, or better, of the transference neurosis. But it is implied. The second criterion, that "so much internal resistance [be] conquered, that there is no need to fear a repetition of the pathological processes," is practically synonomous with the requirement that the transference neurosis be resolved. In many other places Freud does explicitly state that the resolution of the transference is the single most important criterion for successful termination—for instance, when he states that the transference neurosis "is the ground on which the victory must be won, the final expression of which is lasting recovery from the neurosis" (Freud, 1912, p. 108).

The third criterion for termination indicates that the analysand has learned enough about the psychoanalytic quest to be able to go on resolving conflicts on his or her own. It is not that the unconscious has been completely revealed, but that the analysand can continue the exploration without the analyst's assistance. This is not so much a restatement of the second criterion as it is a mechanism for the accomplishment of a lasting cure— that is, if the ex-analysand keeps up the analytic exploration as conflicts arise, a return of the original neurotic state of breakdown is not so likely.

Does this mean that Freud viewed the psychoanalytic cure as

permanent? Does this mean that, for Freud, psychoanalysis was a once-in-a-lifetime venture that, if successful, would resolve some set of core issues so that the ex-analysand would be able to go on alone with a life that, while certainly not free of crises and transient regressions just because old inner conflicts had been resolved, would move along in a manageable fashion? These are complicated questions, which Freud spends much of the remainder of this essay addressing. He talks about the relative strength of traumatic events that occur after termination, the constitutional strength of instincts demanding expression, and the capacity of the ego, bolstered by the course of analysis, to cope with both. In the ideal case, the ego does master the new situation, and thus there is no need for further analysis. Or perhaps, if the success of analysis is not "radical enough," or the change in the structure of the psychic agencies is "only partial," the cure will not be long-lasting. In other words, "we may say that analysis, in claiming to cure neuroses by ensuring control over instinct, is always right in theory but not always right in practice" (Freud, 1937, p. 229).

After Freud explores these three criteria, he goes on to discuss whether the analysis can be generalized to conflicts not active at the time of the treatment. He also questions the ethics of putting stress on the analysand during treatment—by manipulating the transference—to prepare the analysand for later conflicts. He basically feels that the approach would not be effective but that it is certainly proper, and perhaps even helpful, to discuss conflicts that might crop up in the future. It seems Freud is saying that yes, in the ideal case, we can hope for permanent results and a once-in-a-lifetime undertaking. But the variables are so complicated, and the exceptions so numerous, that this is merely a conceptual ideal.

In this essay Freud also explores the issue of the analyst's own analysis. Commenting about countertransference themes, such as an analyst's tendency to evade applying the lessons of analysis to his or her own case by continually applying them to analysands, Freud makes the suggestion that analysts should themselves undergo repeated analyses, at intervals of five years. Of course, analyses lasted several months or a year then, and the five-year interval made sense. Now, with analyses often lasting longer than five years, it is the principle and not the specific time designation that remains useful. In other words, just after discussing the conceptual ideal of a once-in-a-lifetime analysis, Freud makes a distinction when it comes to analysts themselves and suggests that their own analyses cannot be so definitively terminated.

I have taken the time to mention several themes of Freud's one essay specifically about termination because, as will be apparent in future chapters, each of the formulations he presents here will become the starting point for future debates and developments in the field.

A Discrepancy Between Freud's Theory and His Practice

We have seen that Freud's experience with actual terminations sometimes ended disastrously, the reason usually being that he did not pay enough attention to unresolved transference issues and feelings about termination. And yet his theory of termination is brilliantly conceived and has yet to be surpassed— even by modern clinicians who are much more attuned to the practical difficulties of termination. How are we to explain the discrepancy between Freud's practical failure and theoretical lucidity? Of course, many have pointed out that it was part of Freud's genius to make important theoretical advances even in the wake of failed practical experiments. Thus, after the treatment failure with Anna O., Breuer left the practice of psychoanalysis altogether, and it was Freud who culled the critical lesson about transference from the debacle.

But there is another issue here, having to do with countertransference, which may even be a character trait of Freud's. Freud was terrified of dependency—his own on others. Early in his career he tended first to idealize and then to feel disappointed in or even betrayed by colleagues he had held in high esteem. His relationships with Breuer, Wilhelm Fliess, and perhaps even Jung fit this pattern. In his personal correspondence and in recollections by intimates he shows a clear search for total independence. Thus, he remarked once to Ferenczi that, having overcome his homosexuality, he had come to a greater self-dependence (letter to Ferenczi, Oct. 17, 1910, cited in Jones, 1955,

2:420). Ernest Jones reports that when he asked Freud why he was so afraid of old age, the latter responded it was because it made him so dependent on others (Jones, 1955, 2:420). Then there was the fact that Freud, alone among psychoanalysts, was his own analyst. Ernest Becker, discussing this and related biographical facts, concludes that because he was so terrified of both dependency and death, Freud took on the *"causa-sui* project. . . , the attempt to father himself" (Becker, 1973, p. 107). Following Otto Rank's critique of Freud, Becker claims that Freud's overly sexualized theories were defensively formulated to avoid confronting the issue that gave Freud the most difficulty: anxiety about dependency and death.

In addition, Freud's biographers have pointed to his difficulties with partings, his notorious "breaks" with each of the former disciples whose theoretical differences he took as a sign of betrayal, if not of himself, then of "the cause." François Roustang (1982) chronicles the series of mentor-mentee relationships that ended in such breaks, beginning with Jung and Adler, and including Ferenczi, Rank, and Tausk. Each time, Freud felt betrayed, and while publicly debunking the theoretical errors of the errant analyst, privately became more insistent on the need for total self-sufficiency.

Given these personal issues, is it any wonder Freud would miss, in practice, some of the issues his analysands might have about terminating an analysis with him? Consider a hypothetical case: A man enters psychoanalysis with Freud, very depressed, becomes deeply engrossed in the process of joining Freud in making interpretations about his psyche, and in fact a couple of months later is feeling much better in general, is not depressed, and for the first time in his life thinks highly of himself. Then, when Freud decides it is time to terminate, the man suddenly regresses into depression and self-abasement: "He never was interested in me, really, I'm just another of his famous cases, he'll replace me soon enough. I was an idiot to ever have really believed he cared about me."

These are not unusual feelings at the time of termination. Today, the therapist is aware such feelings might arise, and in fact encourages the client to express them. But Freud was less than sensitive to such things. Thus, with the Wolfman, who must have felt abandoned by Freud if Ruth Mack Brunswick is correct in her interpretation of his unresolved murderous wishes toward Freud, Freud merely suggested that he avoid dependency feelings and perhaps give a gift upon leaving.

We know from Abram Kardiner's account (1977) of his analysis with Freud in 1922 that the latter was fairly insensitive to his analysands' feelings in the matter. At the beginning of their encounter, Freud told Kardiner they would meet for a specified length of time. No more mention was made of termination until, at the beginning of a session many months later, Freud informed Kardiner that their last meeting was coming up very soon, as they had agreed. Kardiner was shocked by the news; he remembered their agreement, but "it had simply not registered with me. . . . My analysis terminated on the first of April, 1922. I felt uneasy, reluctant to leave, and, in a way, resentful about it" (p. 67). Freud seems to have done nothing to help him with his feelings about the separation and loss.

Thus Freud could be brilliant in his theoretical discussion of termination—an abstract discussion about when the natural point to end arrives—but he seemed less capable of helping his analysands with their actual feelings about the loss. Later analysts, who lengthened the analytic process by years and fostered more profound regression in their analysands in order to uncover more deeply buried early memories, would discover that the result was greater dependency. They were forced to lengthen the termination as more of an actual weaning of the client from the therapist than as a search for that final bit of shared insight (Saul, 1958). But that development is the topic for the next chapter.

Chapter 2

The Termination
of Psychoanalysis after Freud

THERE ARE two ways to look at developments within psychoanalysis vis-à-vis termination. The first is to review the literature that directly examines termination issues. The second is to step back, look for major trends in the development of psychoanalysis as a theory and practice, and try to understand how those larger issues affect termination. For instance, as we mentioned before, longer analyses tend to deepen dependencies and to make separation a bigger termination issue. Thus this chapter is in two parts: the first deals with specific developments on termination as expressed in the literature, the second with changes in the theory and practice of psychoanalysis that radically alter the meaning of termination.

Before beginning, I should mention that the literature is mainly concerned with theory. It rarely explores personal styles, individual sensibilities, and certain realities of relationships that cannot be translated into theoretical terms. In this regard, it is illuminating to read Harry Guntrip's (1975) account of his two personal analyses, one with Ronald Fairbairn and the other with D. W. Winnicott. Compared to Winnicott's warm, spontaneous approach, Guntrip finds Fairbairn, whom he describes as the greater theoretician of the two, to be very orthodox, formal, and precise in his interpretations. Where Winnicott shook his hand after each session, Fairbairn was much more proper. And yet, at the end of Guntrip's final session with Fairbairn, "I suddenly realized that in all that long period we had never once shaken hands, and he was letting me leave without that friendly gesture. I put out my hand and at once he took it, and I suddenly saw a few tears trickle down his face. I saw the warm heart of this man with a fine mind and a shy nature" (pp. 55-56). Thus therapists have different styles, and feelings are present even when interactions seem rather formal. As we explore the literature, keep in mind that theoretical discussions rarely touch on such subtleties.

The Literature on Termination

Sandor Ferenczi's (1927) early paper on the subject contains comments that are very relevant to termination today. Ferenczi believed it was important to create a sense of timelessness in the consulting room. In this context, timelessness did not refer to the length of the analysis itself. In fact, only by suspending the whole issue and creating a state of timelessness can the analytic work be done. According to Ferenczi, it is even possible for an analysis to be very brief, yet be experienced by the participants as timeless—like the timelessness that exists in the unconscious. In fact, it is the parallel between the timelessness of the treatment and that of the unconscious that permits better contact with the unconscious. When the end of the analysis draws near, the two participants in the timeless encounter have to prepare themselves for a very time-bound departure from their encounter and reenter their respective social worlds. Ferenczi also suggests a criterion for termination: that the analysand be fully capable of free association.

Otto Fenichel (1924) presents the termination of one analysis he conducted. He reports that the woman analysand began to fantasize about birth—not so much giving birth, though that was present—but more about being born, perhaps reborn. The termination was symbolized by birth images in the analysand's unconscious. Fenichel wrote the essay as a comment on the debate then raging on Otto Rank's theory of the birth trauma. It was this theory that Freud was rebutting at the beginning of "Analysis Terminable and Interminable" (1937; see chapter 1). Rank (1924) pictured analysis essentially as a rebirthing. The fetus is in the womb nine months, hence the therapy should last that long too—thereby creating a more womblike context for the rebirthing. Rank's theory of the centrality of the birth trauma in the etiology of adult neuroses was quite controversial. In this essay Fenichel admitted that even one of his analysands was discovering in her unconscious long-repressed birth wishes.

During the years following Freud's pronouncements, very few articles on termination appeared in the *International Journal of Psychoanalysis*, the major outlet for psychoanalytic writing. Perhaps no one wanted to challenge them or create alternative formulations to Freud's. In addition, few had considered the termination phase of analysis as important as it would be a few years later. In 1950, a slew of articles were published in the *Journal*. John Rickman (1950) begins his by summarizing developments in the literature on termination. He lists the criteria for termination,

> in the order in which these criteria have appeared in our periodic literature:
> "(a) the capacity to move smoothly in memory (and to let old feelings surge up on occasion) from the past to the present and back again, i.e. the removal of infantile amnesia, which of course includes a facing and working through of the Oedipus complex
> (b) the capacity for heterosexual genital satisfaction [This requirement has been challenged since, and remains at the center of the debate between feminists and psychoanalysts]
> (c) the capacity to tolerate libidinal frustration and privation without regressive defences, and without anxiety
> (d) the capacity to work and to endure unemployment
> (e) the capacity to tolerate the aggressive impulses in the self and others without losing object love in its full sense and without guilt, and
> (f) the capacity to mourn." (Rickman, 1950, p. 128)

Annie Reich (1950) speaks to the question of resolving the transference. She feels that it is never completely resolved, the analyst always remaining an "overimportant" person, but that the wish to hold onto an infantile relationship with the analyst is slowly relinquished during the course of a successful analysis.

Michael Balint's (1950) contribution to the discussion involves separating into three main issues the criteria for successful termination: (1) the instinctual aims—for instance, Balint, like most analysts of his day, agreed with Freud's formulation in *Three*

Essays on the Theory of Sexuality (1905b) that genital hetero-sexuality was the only normal sexual orientation; (2) relationships with instinctual objects, or object relationships; and (3) the struc-ture of the ego. These latter two criteria, of course, reflect the influence the newer ego-psychology and object-relations schools were having on psychoanalysis by that time.

Debates emerged about the proper technique for termination. Some analysts (Held, 1955; Saul, 1958; Stone, 1961) feel that in order properly to wean the analysand from the consulting room, the analysis should be altered in the termination phase. Perhaps fewer sessions per week and then gradual separation work better with some analysands. Perhaps ending with sessions in which the analysand sits up and faces the analyst would permit the analysand a better handle on who that analyst is, as distinct from who he or she is in the transference. Perhaps some self-reve-lation on the part of the analyst would help with reality testing. But Glover (1955) insists that the analysis, and the basic rule of free association, must proceed right up to the last session—and beyond. Lipton (1961) agrees with Glover that free association and relative deprivation must be the rule until the end, other-wise the analyst would be providing gratifications that would preclude the analysands' continuing the analytic process after termination.

Also explored in the literature is the question of who decides when to terminate? Ferenczi and Rank (1925), Glover (1955), and Rangell (1966) insist it is the analyst who assesses the prog-ress of the treatment and decides when to terminate. Ticho (1972), Kris (1982), and Kohut (1977) would leave it more up to the analysand, the theory being that as the time for termination nears, the analysand, being relatively free of neurotic needs, knows best. Ralph Greenson (1966), in his diplomatic way, combines the two positions in declaring that the decision is a mutual one and that the transference and countertransference needs of both must be analyzed before the termination can be fully agreed upon.

Ticho (1972) makes a substantial contribution to this literature when he distinguishes between the analysand's life goals and the treatment goals. The former are "the goals the patient would seek to attain if he could put his potentialities to use. . . . The treatment goals concern removal of obstacles to the patient's discovery of what his potentialities are" (p. 315). Having made this important distinction, Ticho formulates the natural moment for termination in a new light: "The successful attainment of the treatment goals enables the patient to terminate psychoanalysis and to proceed toward achieving his life goals" (p. 332). The therapist is likely to find this formulation very useful. For instance, there is the client who originally entered therapy claiming that primary relationships were very problematic, then achieves a great deal of personal growth and according to most other criteria is ready to terminate, but is not yet in a satisfying primary relationship. Therapists often err by continuing therapy too long just because that relationship has not been established, or by terminating too precipitously when it has been and claiming success for the treatment, even though all that has happened is that the client's dependency needs—and transference—have been displaced onto the new romantic object. Ticho's formulation provides a way for clinicians to think more deeply about this kind of therapeutic dilemma.

Stephen Firestein offers a useful review of the literature on termination. In his book *Termination in Psychoanalysis* (1978), he lists the generally accepted criteria for termination that he could discern from reading thirty articles by analysts on the subject:

Symptoms have been traced to their genetic conflicts, in the course of which the infantile neurosis has been identified, as the infantile amnesia was undone ("insight"). It is hoped all symptoms have been eliminated, mitigated, or made tolerable. Object relations, freed of transference distortions, have improved, along with the level of psychosexual functioning, the latter attaining "full genitality." Penis envy and castration anxiety have been mastered. The ego is strengthened by virtue of diminishing anachronistic countercathetic formations. The ability to distinguish between fantasy and reality has been sharpened. Acting out has been eliminated. The capacity to tolerate some measure of anxiety and to reduce other unpleasant affects to signal quantities has improved. The ability to tolerate delay of gratification is increased, and along with it there is a shift from autoplastic to alloplastic conflict solutions.

Sublimations have been strengthened, and the capacity to experience pleasure without guilt or other notable inhibiting factors has improved. Working ability, under which so many aspects of ego function, libidinal and aggressive drive gratification are subsumed, has improved. (pp. 226–27)

As you can see, since Freud the list of the criteria for termination has grown longer. Remember, for Freud there were three simple requirements for rightfully terminated analysis: the symptoms are gone, there are signs of deep enough change to make it likely the symptoms will not resurface, and the analysand seems ready to go on in life without the analyst's actual presence. As Rickman (1950) reports, the list has grown from there, and Firestein attempts to bring the list up to date. It may be that the list has grown since Firestein's book was published. In chapter 4 I will discuss some reasons for the growth of the list, but basically, as analysts expand the list of clients and symptoms they believe to be amenable to analysis, probe deeper into the psyche, and lengthen analyses, the list of criteria for termination grows longer.

Firestein's (1978) own study of termination supplies a useful glimpse of the way analysts handle termination today. He first located cases in the New York Psychoanalytic Institute clinic, conducted by candidates in training or younger members of the institute, where a natural termination occurred—"as opposed to those prematurely interrupted for extraneous reasons." He then interviewed the treating clinician and the supervising analyst about the case and the progress of the termination, as well as getting supplementary opinions about each case from senior analysts, and, where possible, interviewing the analysands after termination. He presents eight cases in some detail, one of which I will briefly summarize.

Frank B. was thirty-two when he entered an eight-year analysis. He was married and had two children. Part of the reason he entered analysis was that his wife had recently done so. He complained of an inability to urinate in public, feelings of inadequacy and childishness, frequent masturbation, and sexual difficulties including impotence with his wife, except when he fantasized during intercourse about a man defecating.

His mother, obsessed about cleanliness, had until he was six accompanied him to the bathroom to make sure he defecated properly. She washed his penis until he was four. In fact, later in the analysis he remembered her taking him to the bathroom to clean him up after he wet or defecated in his pants and his getting an erection when she touched him. In regard to his father, he remembered at age five watching him have a bowel movement and feeling a sense of awe and a tingling in his penis. At about that time, he later recalled, an adult male visitor in the house seduced him to masturbate him in the bathroom.

He and his older brother, with whom he competed and to whom he felt inferior, went to the bathroom together until he was thirteen. He described himself as a sissy in school, with no friends. He entered the military at nineteen and there began the practice of masturbating in lavatories, often with fantasies of a man defecating. Early in his analysis he arrived at the interpretation that he feared urinating in public because another man might notice his state of excitement. His equating of penis and feces was explored, as were his homosexual feelings and his wish for anal penetration by his father. The analysis was long and difficult. With repeated interpretation of links between childhood events and his current sexual difficulties and feelings of inadequacy, he slowly began to advance in his professional career and to have satisfactory intercourse with his wife without the defecation fantasies.

But the transference was heavily erotized. He reported fantasies about sex with his male analyst, and accompanying anxiety. He was jealous of the analyst's wife, and he masturbated in the analyst's toilet. In the middle of the analysis he moved so that it took him an hour each way to drive to sessions. Still, he derived sufficient gratification from the analysis to continue. He seemed even to enjoy the frequent outbursts of rage toward the analyst, for instance, when the latter announced a vacation. The symptoms improved up to a point, but he never expressed any gratitude toward the analyst, and the erotized transference did not seem to be resolving.

A number of events brought the analyst to the decision to suggest termination. There was a lack of progress in resolving the transference. The long drive to the appointment took three hours out of Frank's day, and his wife was complaining about the time drain. He had a new and better job. And the analyst felt the analysand may have derived maximal benefit from the analysis. The analyst and his supervisor felt the fact that Frank had for the first time not flown into a rage when the previous vacation had been announced might mean he could tolerate termination. Termination was discussed for about a year, a date was set, and there were several more months of working through the impending separation. After the date was finally set, Frank's associations turned to giving the analyst a gift, perhaps one of the art pieces he created in his spare time. He asked a lot of questions about the possibility of returning if he ran into trouble. Some previously unmentioned childhood memories cropped up, and he became aware for the first time of how much guilt he felt about masturbation. He worried about how he would mourn for the lost analyst, and felt sad. Nevertheless he acted in a more mature and contemplative fashion than he had during most of the analysis, and the two parted without the kind of storm that had accompanied earlier partings.

At the follow-up by Firestein two years later it was learned that more severe reactions had followed the last session. Frank continued to do well in his career and seemed to have made and maintained some friendships. But he felt entirely abandoned by his analyst, full of rage and depressed. He became impotent once again and resorted again to the male defecation fantasies during intercourse. His depression, and increasing self-centeredness, led him to return to see his analyst on several occasions, but each time he found him distant and the meeting very unsatisfactory. Eventually he went to see another psychiatrist closer to his home and was seeing him sporadically at the time of the follow-up.

Although this was not an entirely successful outcome, the case highlights some important issues regarding termination. There was the unresolved transference. (Perhaps the analyst was collusive in this—he did see Frank for one dollar per session even though Frank eventually made a good salary and his wife worked.) There was a regression in response to abandonment feelings at termination. And the associations of the termination phase are fairly frequently heard fantasies—wanting to give the analyst a gift, concerns about how the mourning might usefully occur, and so forth.

Interestingly, this case resembles that of the Wolfman in many respects. Both analysands had problems about homosexuality and had experienced seduction, anal erotism, and intense gratification from being in analysis. In both cases the analyst had been willing to receive little if any fee. Frank also exhibited some obsessional traits, had witnessed the primal scene at a very early age, and could only be potent with his wife in the position Freud characterized as *a tergo*. In both cases, the transference was not really resolved. I do not want to make too much of the similarities between the two cases. What is relevant is the greater attention that the analyst Firestein interviewed gave to termination themes. Remember, Freud was aware of the issue—he suggested that the Wolfman give him a gift—but he did not give enough attention or time to the themes, so the Wolfman never really terminated, he only went through the motions, and perhaps that merely to gain the great master's favor and ensure himself a spot as fellow-traveler in the community of psychoanalysts. Today, analyst and supervisor plan terminations very carefully, precisely in order to avoid the kind of failed termination that occurred in Frank B.'s case.

From the eight cases, Firestein draws a series of conclusions, a few of which I will note here: First, there is an identifiable phase at the termination of an analysis. Second, there are affective reactions on the part of the analysand. Third, relatively typical fantasies and wishes emerge, and the resistances, new themes, and memories that appear are usually familiar from earlier phases of the analysis. Fourth, symptoms often reappear during the termination phase. Fifth, the work of analysis usually continues on after the termination. Sixth, the way the analysand handled earlier announcements of the analyst's vacations can offer clues to how the termination will be handled. And finally, the analyst's own experience of terminating his or her didactic analysis influences the course of the current analysis being terminated. These are certainly modest claims after the reporting of some very rich and detailed case material. But what is impressive is that empirical data are thoughtfully presented, and the conclusions are warranted by the data. All of Firestein's conclusions about the termination of psychoanalysis apply as well to the termination of psychotherapy.

The last topic I will mention in this review is the distinction analysts make between therapeutic analyses (the ones they practice to alleviate their client's symptoms), and didactic analyses (those they must undergo as part of their training). Early training analyses were quite informal. Thus, Balint (1954, reported in Weigert, 1955) describes Eitingon's training analysis with Freud in 1909; the two took walks twice a week after supper for a while, and then Eitingon went off to Berlin to practice. Typically, Freud concentrated on insight into unconscious themes and ignored or minimized the idealization and dependency that might develop in the therapeutic relationship. And in many cases, this was perfectly appropriate. Thus Joseph Wortis (1954), an American psychiatrist, reports on his several-month didactic analysis with Freud, which ended cheerfully enough, with Freud offering him a signed copy of one of his books as he departed. There was no need, as there might have been in Kardiner's didactic analysis (see chapter 1), to talk of Wortis's feelings about separation.

But Freud was well aware of how the special circumstance of the analysand's being an analyst might complicate the didactic experience, or, more relevant to this discussion, make it virtually interminable. This is why Freud (1937) recommends periodic reanalysis for every analyst. Other analysts express similar concerns. Balint (1954) proposes that the trainee's analyst must get past the trainee's need to idealize the analyst and make concerted attempts to free up the negative transference as well as the deep-lying dependency needs if the didactic analysis is to be a success. Weigert (1955) also feels the danger is that the novitiate might cling to idealizations of, and dependencies on, the more senior training analyst, especially since the two will be members of the same psychoanalytic institute, so that the goal of the didactic analysis must be "a mutually respectful differentiation" (p. 273).

Others conclude that didactic analyses, by their very nature, are interminable. Ekstein (1965) wonders openly if this is not the case. Marion Milner (1950) expresses the concern very succinctly: "Perhaps we, as analysts, are handicapped in knowing all about what ending feels like, for by the mere fact of becoming analysts we have succeeded in bypassing an experience which our patients have to go through. We have chosen to identify ourselves with our analyst's profession and to act out that identification" (p. 191). This concern will be important in the discussion that follows, not only because psychotherapists are likely to experience the same interminable quality in their personal therapies but also because the modern community of therapy consumers creates a culture that likewise fosters interminable therapy.

Thus the post-Freudian psychoanalytic lilterature on termination basically remains true to Freud's original formulation—with a few deviations here and there—and what proliferates in the literature is really just more detailed descriptions of how the date is to be set and the termination phase to proceed. Herbert Gaskill (1980) sums up the position of many analysts today: "Freud's suggestion that an analysis is complete when the ego has attained its maximal psychological capacity for functioning seems as relevant now as it was in 1937" (p. 21).

Developments in Analytic Practice as a Whole

It is not easy to characterize developments in psychoanalysis, since in the course of its development analysis splits into so many schools of thought. Nevertheless, I will attempt to list a few major shifts in psychoanalytic theory, identifying trends in general enough terms to include the schools that still consider themselves Freudian, whether they emphasize ego psychology, object relations, self psychology, or phenomenology. Of course, by speaking in such general terms I will be leaving out the particulars that distinguish the various schools.

At this level of generality, I think it fair to say that since Freud's death, there have been seven noticeable shifts in the preoccupations of psychoanalytic theory:

1. Analysts have tended to enlarge on the variety and depth of psychopathology that they consider amenable to analytic treatment (Stone, 1954). Thus, while Freud felt he could not treat schizophrenic patients because their intense narcissism prevented the development of sufficient transference, the next generation of analysts attempted just such treatment and revised an-

alytic theory to fit their enlarged practical experience. Likewise, Freud at first aimed to treat only the neurosis and leave the underlying character structure essentially intact. Later in his career, influenced by Reich (1933), Freud attempted alterations of the character structure, but he was relatively pessimistic about the prognosis. Freud eventually broke with Reich, supposedly because of the latter's membership in the Communist Party, but also because of theoretical differences such as Reich's rejection of the death instinct (Reich, 1967; Robinson, 1969). Still, Reich's concept of character analysis was incorporated into orthodox psychoanalytic thinking.

Today analysts are willing to undertake the treatment of very severe psychoses and character disorders. Boyer and Giovacchini (1967, 1980) advocate psychoanalysis with patients with schizophrenic, borderline, and characterological disorders. In the preface to the second edition of *Psychoanalytic Treatment of Schizophrenia, Borderline and Characterological Disorders* (1980), they mention that prior to the publication of the first edition, few analysts attempted to work with severely disturbed analysands. But since that time, many analysts have discovered that "the analysis of some schizophrenic patients and character disorders can be a gratifying experience" (p. xii).

2. The prototype for understanding both the development of symptomatology and the evolution of the transference has shifted to an earlier stage of childhood. Where Freud focused almost exclusively on the oedipal drama involving the three- to five-year-old child and the two parents, current discussions are more likely to focus on an earlier stage, such as infancy. The focus has shifted from oedipal to preoedipal issues. And it is no longer always the triangle of child, mother, and father that warrants the closest scrutiny, but rather the dyad of mother and infant. Melanie Klein (1950), who figured prominently in this theoretical shift, discusses the implications for termination: "Before terminating an analysis I have to ask myself whether the conflicts and anxieties experienced during the first year of life have been sufficiently analyzed and worked through in the course of the treatment" (p. 78).

3. While Freud looked for the singular traumas of childhood upon which one became fixated for life, later analysts would look

for the recurrent patterns of early object relations that shaped later character structure. Thus, it would be the day-to-day relationship between infant and mother rather than the single moment of intense grief that would matter most in the etiology of the current emotional disorder. For many analysts, the mother-infant relationship becomes the prototype of later difficulties in relationships, and the model for the therapeutic relationship. Winnicott (1965) writes:

> My thesis is that what we do in therapy is to attempt to imitate the natural process that characterizes the behaviour of any mother of her own infant. If I am right, it is the mother-infant couple that can teach us the basic principles on which we may base our therapeutic work, when we are treating children whose early mothering was "not good enough," or was interrupted. (pp. 19-20)

4. Where Freud stressed insight—that is, the anamnesis—in the overcoming of symptoms, and only later became convinced of the importance of working through the transference neurosis, later analysts would place more emphasis on the therapeutic relationship as a healing experience and would view the attainment of insight as just one facet of that relationship. The ongoing analysis of transference and countertransference is of course another important facet, but so is the experiencing of the therapeutic relationship itself, whether one conceptualizes that as a "corrective emotional experience" (Alexander, 1952) or, as Loewald (1960) does, as a reworking of the parent-child relationship:

> The parent-child relationship can serve as a model here. The parent ideally is in an empathic relationship of understanding the child's particular stage in development, yet ahead in his vision of the child's future and mediating this vision to the child in his dealing with him. This vision, informed by the parent's own experience and knowledge of growth and future is, ideally, a more articulate and more integrated version of the core of being that the child presents to the parent. This "more" that the parent sees and knows, he mediates to the child so that the child in identification with it can grow. . . . In

analysis, if it is to be a process leading to structural changes, interactions of a comparable nature have to take place. (p. 229)

Kohut's (1971, 1977) idea that the analyst's empathy heals the narcissistic client's deeply wounded self puts him squarely at the forefront of this development. This is discussed at greater length in chapter 4.

5. There is a shift of focus to more primitive defense mechanisms. Freud focused on repression and some of its derivatives, like reaction formation and sublimation. As later analysts shifted their attention to earlier phases of child development, they concomitantly concentrated on the more primitive kinds of defensive maneuvers the younger child or infant would employ: denial, splitting, projection, and projective identification. Then they began to look for the more primitive mechanisms they assumed to be prior to, and hidden beneath, mature defenses like repression. James Grotstein (1981) articulates this view: "Splitting . . . and projective identification . . . comprise the lowest common denominator of all defense mechanisms as well as of all perceptions and thought processes through varying differentiations, displacements, and secondary recombinations. Ultimately, repression, denial, isolation, doing-undoing, intellectualization, identification with the aggressor, etc., are combinations of splitting and projective-identifications" (p. 136).

6. The shifts in theory that were inspired by the treatment of more severely disturbed patients—including the focus on earlier childhood relationships and the attention to more primitive defense mechanisms—were meanwhile applied to the more functional analysands, those whom Freud might have deemed neurotic, and the result has been that analysts probe more deeply into the psyches of the latter, seeking to touch the infantile or psychotic layers they feel certain must be hidden deep within even the most sane individual. Again, Melanie Klein was the pathbreaker here. André Green (1975) comments on this development:

Freud's implied model of neurosis is based on perversion (neurosis as negative of perversion). . . . The implied model of neurosis *and* of perversion is nowadays based on psychosis. . . . And this is also why some analysts write that an analysis of a neurosis is not complete until the psychotic layer is reached. . . . When at last we reach the psychotic core we find what we may well call the patient's private madness, and this may be one reason why interest is now shifting towards borderline states. (p. 5)

7. Analyses last longer. Partly, this is a logical correlate of the first six issues I've discussed. It simply takes longer to treat more serious and deeper-lying psychopathology, or to delve more deeply into the psychotic core of relatively healthy individuals. Janet Malcolm (1981) sums it up: "In the twenties, one to two years was deemed sufficient; in the thirties and forties, two to four years was the norm; in the fifites and sixties, four to six years; today, six to eight" (p. 151). Freud was concerned about the possibility that psychoanalysis would become interminable. Schmideberg (1938) cautioned colleagues that, if an analysis runs for longer than six years, the analyst must examine possible countertransference themes that postpone termination, and there is a real danger that the prolonged analysis will cause the patient to be estranged from reality. Still analyses continued to lengthen. By now, eight to ten years is not considered excessive in some psychoanalytic institutes.

What effect do these developments have on the termination of analysis? Obviously, as analyses grow longer, probe deeper, and aim to alter more firmly fixed psychic structure, termination becomes a more critical phase of the treatment and there is a larger potential for negative repercussions of poorly navigated terminations. Partly this is because of the greater dependency and regression that are fostered in the analytic situation—that is, the analyst purposely fosters a certain amount of dependency so that sufficient regression will occur for the analysand to be in touch with all those primitive fantasies. Then too, the more severely disturbed people who are now judged to be suitable for psychoanalysis, on the average, have more difficulty with separation and loss.

Psychoanalysts are well aware of these issues. Consider the

debate I mentioned about the clinical management of the termination phase. One side says that toward the end of the analysis, the analyst should become more self-revealing, the frequency of sessions should be gradually reduced, and the last several sessions should be conducted face-to-face so that the analysand has a better opportunity to phase out the intensive process. The other side insists that the basic rule—and the basic format, including the couch and the analyst's neutrality—must be continued right up to the end.

The analysts who argue the former position are essentially suggesting the analysand be weaned from analysis, just as the infant is weaned from the breast. But those who argue the latter position do not necessarily consider termination issues any less important. They merely believe that rigorous interpretation, and not weaning, is the way to manage the oral-dependency needs, the fantasies of merging with a powerful parental figure, or the rage and despair about abandonment that regularly arise at the time of termination, particularly if an analysis has been long and has touched on primitive layers of the psyche. Melanie Klein (1950), while insisting that infantile issues be worked through before termination is contemplated, includes in that working through the achievement of the capacity to mourn. Then, as part of the work of termination, she suggests the analyst help the analysand with the process of mourning for the "here and now" relationship itself.

Where Freud could spend months or years uncovering repressed memories and then merely announce to the Wolfman or to Abram Kardiner that it is time to terminate, and perhaps suggest that they not give in too much to their dependency needs or that they give him a gift as a symbolic parting gesture, the issue of termination looms much larger for the psychoanalyst today—and requires more careful attention. Rather than pursuing the themes that are or should be explored and worked through in the course of terminating an analysis, I will shift gears and discuss psychotherapy, where the same termination issues regularly come up, and where the lessons of psychoanalysis are usefully applied.

Chapter 3

The Termination
of Psychotherapy Today

PHILIP RIEFF (1968), in discussing "the triumph of the therapeutic," writes: "At its best, psychoanalytic therapy is devoted to the long and dubious task of rubbing a touch of that analytic genius into less powerful minds" (p. 30). Today, it is more often psychotherapy, not psychoanalysis, that carries on the task. Therapy, because it is less expensive and less time-consuming, is accessible to more people, and many would say that intensive, long-term therapy, when it is informed by psychoanalytic theory, can accomplish as much as psychoanalysis. I will begin by briefly explaining what I mean by psychoanalytically informed therapy. With so many varieties of therapy available today it helps to clarify. I will first demonstrate how psychoanalytic principles can guide a psychotherapy, then present a case, and finally continue the clinical discussion of termination that I began in the context of psychoanalytic thought. The context, however, will have shifted from the psychoanalytic to the psychotherapeutic consulting room. By way of illustration, I will present two additional cases. I will conclude the chapter with a brief discussion of countertransference and termination.

Up to this point, I have presented clinical issues and cases drawn mainly from the professional literature. This is because I am not a psychoanalyst. A psychiatrist, I was trained by analysts to practice psychotherapy, and I will illustrate how psychoanalytic theory continues to inform my practice. But I cannot present a firsthand account of psychoanalytic practice. Psychotherapy is a different matter. From now on, I will present my own understanding of how therapy is practiced, and my own cases.

If, because of variations among schools of thought, it is difficult to describe trends in psychoanalysis, it is doubly difficult to portray how therapy is theorized and practiced, there being so many idiosyncratic approaches and no official institutes to foster orthodoxy. Therefore I will attempt to describe what I understand to be trends among practitioners. This means that many of my formulations do not reflect any particular body of literature, since, for the most part, practitioners tend to borrow from various schools of thought. Also, most therapists do not publish their own work and ideas, making it even more difficult to assess what occurs in the average therapist's practice. Nevertheless, I will attempt to present principles of termination in terms general enough to make sense to practitioners of various theoretical persuasions. In this chapter I will discuss long-term, open-ended therapy. Brief therapy is also informed by psychoanalysis, as I will explain in chapter five.

Psychoanalysis and Psychotherapy

The majority of contemporary therapists borrow from psychoanalysis, adapting it to the idiom of the face-to-face encounter. Frieda Fromm-Reichmann (1950) states the goal of intensive psychotherapy:

"Alleviation of patients' emotional difficulties in living and elimination of the symptomatology, this goal to be reached by gaining insight into, and understanding of the unconscious roots of patients' problems, the genetics and dynamics, on the part of both patient and psychiatrist, whereby such understanding and insight may frequently promote changes in the dynamic structure of the patient's personality." (p. x)

There are discussions among psychoanalysts about what differentiates psychoanalysis from psychotherapy (Nemetz, 1979; Wallerstein, 1969). Ticho (1970) identifies three significant differences: the free-association technique and couch employed in psychoanalysis foster deeper regression; the analyst is "neutral" and avoids becoming a model, whereas the therapist is more of a model, is more active in the encounter, and does a certain amount of "reeducation"; and the analyst makes only insight-producing interventions, while the therapist might also give advice, be supportive, and so forth. According to Ticho, psychotherapy can accomplish as much in terms of symptom reduction but results in less resolution of unconscious conflict and less autonomy. Merton Gill (1954) suggests that the crucial ingredient that differentiates psychoanalytic psychotherapy from other therapeutic approaches is the therapist's persistent focus on interpretations of the transference. Lifschutz (1984) agrees with Gill, and would even call all other forms of therapy by some other name, for instance, "counseling." My own view is that in many cases psychoanalytic psychotherapy can incorporate more varied forms of intervention and still accomplish as deep and lasting change as can psychoanalysis.

Wallerstein (1969) describes a continuum, with psychoanalysis at one end and supportive psychotherapy or counseling at the other. In the middle is expressive, or insight-producing, psychotherapy, which is the same as psychoanalytically informed psychotherapy. Kernberg (1984) employs the same continuum. Robert Langs (1973, 1974) presents a concise and rigorous outline of technique, though I find his instructions rigid in places, and his style more formal than my own. Dewald (1964) and Malan (1979) present quite accessible guides for the practitioner.

As an example of how a psychoanalytic principle can inform and be adapted to psychotherapy, consider the link Freud made between idea and affect. In his essay on the unconscious, Freud (1915) explains that affect cannot be repressed. Only the idea or memory trace of an experience is repressed and lodged in the unconscious. If the analyst guesses what resides in the analysand's unconscious and tells the analysand about it, the insight does little good. It is merely an intellectual observation. When the analysand is able to connect idea with affect, what was unconscious becomes accessible to consciousness, and the analysis proceeds. This is the analytic principle.

Any therapist who has worked with a bright and highly intellectual client knows that this task is not as easy as it might appear. One such client, a man in his mid-thirties, listened intently during one session as I explained to him how his early feelings of neglect and betrayal by a self-indulgent mother might have something to do with his current problem in sharing his feelings with a woman. He thought about what I said, seemed to make some links with conflicts that were troubling him in a particular relationship, and left my office seeming less anxious than when he had arrived. A week later he walked in and announced that everything I had said the week before was true, but not helpful, since it was all "purely intellectual." He told me he did not think he was making much progress in therapy with me, and he was thinking of quitting and going to see another therapist who did "body work." "At least that's not so intellectual and unfeeling."

I asked this client how he felt about my being so "purely intellectual." He began to tell me that it might be helpful for some people but that he had already done a lot of thinking about himself, and he did not think my interpretations added much new. I asked if he might not also be feeling misunderstood. After all, he was pouring out his heart to me, and all I was giving him back were intellectual interpretations. He agreed, and seemed to relax a little. Then he listed some other complaints he had about me: I was too formal at the beginning of sessions; I never answered with much content when he asked me how I was, while I expected him to come forth with all kinds of "deep emotional problems"; and I never really gave him much advice about what to do about his problems—I just made those interpretations.

This client's report is accurate. I do not say much when a client asks how I am, I try not to give much advice, and I try to offer useful interpretations. I acknowledged all that. Then I explained that our task was to look at his situation. If I used his time with me to express my problems and conflicts, wouldn't he feel he was not getting my full attention to his concerns? And wasn't it more important for me to help him decide what course he wanted to take rather than what course would please me? I repeated that I understood his concern that I was not present and attentive in more than an intellectual manner. During the ensuing discussion, he reminisced about his father's tendency to pretend to be listening to him, while really thinking of other things, and then to give him advice that usually turned out to be wrong, or at least not matched very closely to his experience.

The client spontaneously made the connection between the current tension in our therapeutic relationship and resentment toward his father that he had been suppressing for years. I reminded him of his complaint that I was too intellectual and pointed out that what was not merely intellectual was the set of strong feelings he had about me, and the feelings about his father that were called up. Was I, like his father, offering him advice that would turn out to be wrong? The link with the transference is very often what makes it possible for a client to connect idea with affect. The "here and now" (Strachey, 1934) experience with the therapist touches conflictual or repressed memories of very early experiences with important others, and since the here-and-now experience involves affects as well as ideas, real contact with the repressed idea becomes possible. This is just one example of how psychoanalytic principles inform the practice of therapy.

But therapy, no matter how informed by the psychoanalytic approach, is not the same as analysis. Consider, for example, the question of eye contact. Some clients refuse to look the therapist in the eye. The therapist must decide whether and when to mention this. If the therapist says something too early, the client might feel she or he is intrusive. The therapist can alter the boundary arrangement significantly by looking directly at the client or looking away. When a client is ready to examine how she or he distances the therapist, the therapist can diminish the distance by maintaining eye contact. When a client's ego seems fragile and the therapist's direct gaze seems to heighten the client's anxiety, the therapist might choose to look away. The whole phenomenon can occur without discussion, or can be examined as another instance of the client's conflicts about trust and closeness. Therapy is no less a "talking cure" if, in the midst of the conversation, or during the silences, the therapist is aware of how eye contact or lack of eye contact intensifies or relaxes the encounter, and how certain clients need more or less intense interaction at one or another moment.

The therapist learns from Freud, and then adapts what has been learned to a new context. Whatever the modern therapist's style—and mine is reflected in the cases presented here—where there are gaps in Freud's method the therapist must improvise. For instance, Freud (1913) admitted: "I cannot bear to be gazed at for eight hours a day (or more). Since, while I listen, I resign myself to the control of my conscious thoughts, I do not wish my expression to give the patient indications which he may interpret or which may influence him in his communications" (p. 134). It is one thing for the analyst, sitting out of view behind the couch, to hide actual personal reactions so that he or she can ascertain how the analysand on the couch fantasizes the analyst might feel. It is quite another for a therapist to try to hide feelings while sitting face to face with a client, particularly when the client complains: "My father always pretended he wasn't angry even when I knew he was, and then later, still denying he was mad, he'd say something sarcastic. I knew I could never get a straight answer out of him about how he was feeling." While it is unfair and counterproductive for the therapist to burden the client with the full force of his feelings and unprocessed reactions, the client's demands for a more human face are also important.

It would simplify matters greatly if someone were to prove that therapists who sit impassively and rely mainly on interpretation are the most effective, while those who show their feelings, those who empathize and actively support, and those who chat and give outright advice are less effective. But no one can really show this to be the case. The direct transposition of psychoanalytic principles into psychotherapy does not necessarily result in the most effective therapeutic practice. Each therapist evolves his or her own style. Still, the lessons of psychoanalysis do apply, so that even in the midst of expressing feelings, talking, making self-revelations, supporting, advising, or even cajoling, the therapist repeatedly discovers anew that the greatest therapeutic gains occur when affect and idea are connected through the interpretation of the transference. A clinical vignette might prove useful here.

Sandra

Sandra could not tell me a precise reason why she was seeking therapy. "Things are just not right for me." She told me during our first session that she felt more comfortable when I asked questions. At thirty-six, she had built a successful professional career for herself but was concerned because she had never been in a lasting primary relationship and in fact had no real friends. From the start I found that I could ask any question I liked—

about her sexual fantasies, thoughts about suicide, envy of her sister, or resentment toward me—and she would give me a frank, revealing answer. But the answer would be curt and to the point. Then she would revert to silence. She offered very few spontaneous utterances, in spite of my requests that she tell me what was on her mind.

During the first several months of therapy, I asked many questions. I found that to be the only way to keep the conversation going, and when there was prolonged silence, her anxiety level rose and the distance between us grew. She seemed to be training me to ask the questions and then, possibly because this convinced her she had some control in our encounter, she was able to be quite candid. (For a discussion of silence, see Masud Khan, 1963.)

After this pattern had become clearly established, I told her I found it remarkable that she required me to ask all the questions but then would be willing to tell me such intimate things about herself. She thought about this for several minutes, then said: "As long as you ask we aren't really talking about what's on my mind. I'll answer all the questions you want." She might as well have added: "But I won't let you know which ones really matter." Characteristically, Sandra's perceptions proved that though she was silent, her mind was rarely still.

Sandra had always felt ignored by her parents. "They treated me like a piece from their fabulous art collection, parading me out to display to people who came to see their expensive collection. But they never cared how I felt the whole time." Sandra feared that if she shared what was on her mind she would be humiliated, as she was when her parents and their guests ignored what she said, or laughed at her when she said something inappropriate. I ventured: "So you prevented your being made into a dead piece of art by disappearing from the room, becoming silent." She agreed. In the months that followed, she began to answer questions more spontaneously, to interject more thoughts into the silences, and to accept more responsibility for maintaining the flow of our conversations.

We explored her feelings about the fact that her mother never viewed her as a separate, unique person, with her own rights, feelings, and wishes. She had to be "mother's good little girl," or her mother became icy and distant. She decided early to comply and be "mother's good little girl." (For a discussion of the ramifications of this kind of compliance, see Miller, 1981). She did well in school, joined all the right social cliques so that she was viewed as a "popular girl," and followed the rules about curfew and dress code. She did break some of the rules—for example, when she drank and became sexually active in her mid-teens—but her parents never found out about that. She remained in their eyes the model child, and her success in her profession was proof.

Intellectual exchanges with her mother were a "disaster."

> She would take me to a bookstore, and I would look around. Each time I selected a book I liked, she would laugh in a mocking way and say, "That book is really pedestrian!" Then she'd show me a book she thought I would like better. I learned to just accept the books she wanted me to read, and forget about my own taste. At least then she wouldn't make fun of me. Even now, when I go home to visit, she buys me books that she thinks are worthy, usually that I don't like, but I read them while I'm there, and then when I get back here I put them in a box in the closet and read what I like. But when I go back for another visit I hurriedly read a few of the books she bought me so she won't get angry.

Sandra was terrified that in the presence of anyone she let really matter to her, she would be treated like a piece from her parents' fabulous art collection. Her dread was circular. In order to avoid what she dreaded, she reproduced it. She assumed I was just like her mother and would make her into another specimen in my collection of successful cures—if she let me. So she would not give me an opportunity to prove I was trustworthy. Every time I guessed what might be occurring in her inner world, she refused to respond, maintaining an icy silence. I had to ask more questions and receive more curt replies. I ended up feeling that I was being negated, my feelings ignored. She was doing to me what had been done to her, out of fear I would do the same again to her.

Once, while I was in the midst of a painful argument with my wife, worried about a crisis in a son's life, and feeling insecure about the quality of therapy I was practicing, I made an interpretation that I was quite sure hit the mark. Sandra said nothing, and there was no change in her expression. I asked; "Why do you refuse to let me know how my interpretations affect you? Even if they're wrong, I know you must have some reaction."

She did not respond. I felt impotent, humiliated, and angry. Because I was not coping too well with my own worries and insecurities that day, I failed to analyze my own countertransference first, and instead responded in anger: "You use your silence to defeat me. You want me to feel as impotent as you!" I knew as soon as I said it that this was a retaliatory attack, and though quite likely true, not a usable interpretation. Sandra was silent for the rest of the session, and we both felt very uncomfortable.

The next week, Sandra came in and said she felt angry and hurt after the last session. This was the first time she had opened a session by spontaneously expressing feelings, and probably the first time she took responsibility for maintaining continuity in our encounter by referring back to something that occurred in a previous session. I had thought about the way my countertransference had interfered with my work during the previous session, and I had independently decided not to make any more angry accusations in the guise of interpretations. When she told me about her feelings, I thanked her for doing so, said she was right, and apologized. Sandra seemed to relax and told me she had thought about what I had said, and I was right, too. She did have trouble acknowledging my helpful interventions. But she felt threatened. The more she trusted me and the closer she felt to me, the more she dreaded total failure and humiliation— and then there was the ultimate trauma that was always hanging over our relationship: if she really let me matter, someday I would leave her and it would really hurt. For the first time, the termination issue was consciously seeping into our work: if she showed me how the therapy was benefiting her, and how much improvement there was in her everyday life, then I would say the work of therapy was done and we must part.

Nothing changed dramatically, but in the ensuing sessions Sandra spoke a little more spontaneously, and we were able to talk about how hard relationships were for her—and partings. Yet she was so tired of being totally alone. Sandra's course in therapy is a good example of how precedents of termination issues surface right from the beginning of therapy. Before proceeding to a presentation of the termination phase of Sandra's therapy, I will make some general comments about the termination of psychotherapy.

The Termination of Psychotherapy

David Cooper (1970) offers a useful metaphor for the termination of psychoanalytic psychotherapy:

> At the commencement of therapy the room may hold hundreds of people, principally all the person's family over several generations, but also significant other people. Some of the population inevitably includes the therapist's internalized others— but the guarantee of good therapy is that the therapist is familiar enough with the machinations of his internal family and has them well enough tamed. Bit by bit in therapy, one identifies the members of this vast family and all its extensions and asks them, appropriately enough, to "leave the room," until one is left with two people who are free to meet or to leave each other. (p. 5)

Everyone experiences repeated losses and separations throughout life, and each person evolves a personal style for coping with the inevitability of loss. Generally, the individual's reasons for seeking therapy have something to do with an unbearable loss, real or imagined, in the past or threatened in the future, or the reasons have something to do with what is dysfunctional or disturbing about the personal style of coping. Some people are so frightened of being rejected or deserted that they withdraw from all meaningful intimacies and consequently feel isolated and alone. Others keep their intimacies superficial in order to avoid the pain that would otherwise follow loss, drift from one superficial relationship to another, and then complain to therapists that they feel empty inside and are bored in all their human encounters (perhaps including this one with the therapist).

Others act helpless, chronically sick, or hopelessly depressed, clinging to whoever comes close, as if hoping that some very powerful and loving individual will come along who will take care of them forever. They might fall apart when a loved one, feeling engulfed, leaves them. Or they might complain to a therapist that they feel merged and lack autonomy and a sense of self. Thus a woman client complains to me that she feels she is merged to a clingy man, lacks her own identity, and gives herself away too much to him, but is afraid to establish more appropriate boundaries for fear she will lose him and be all alone. Others become anxious, dysfunctional, or even psychotic when confronted with a real or potential separation. And others are so consumed with rage toward loved ones who have disappointed or deserted them in the past that they bring into every new relationship an intensity of hostility and ambivalence that precludes the establishment of real intimacy.

Whatever the client's idiosyncratic issues and defensive maneuvers, she or he will bring them into the therapeutic relationship where, one hopes, they can be examined and worked through. The client does not encounter the separation issue only once at the end of therapy any more than one ponders the experience of death only once at the end of life. In regard to death, it is the mortifying losses, the unbearable pains, and all the other little deaths that occur throughout life that provide the conceptual building blocks for our ideas about what awaits us in the end. Likewise, in therapy, the little separations and betrayals that occur during the course of therapy present the client and therapist with an opportunity to understand and work through the client's troublesome issues with separation and loss. A harsh criticism by the therapist, a betrayal, or a rejection will hurt—and probably hurt in the same way as formative unbearable criticisms and rejections once hurt. The criticism might be a figment of the client's imagination projected onto a therapist who was truly not feeling critical at that moment, or the therapist may for some reason have been critical. The sense of rejection might occur when the therapist announces a vacation, or the betrayal might involve the therapist's inability to make life easier for the client fast enough. The real basis of the client's feeling is not the only issue. The therapist must also help the client learn to survive and live fully in face of this risk of disappointment and pain. Then the client will be better able to shed outdated defensive maneuvers. In this way the client prepares for the real loss—of the therapist—that awaits at the end of the therapeutic encounter.

Margaret Mahler (1972) identifies the paradox of termination: in order to individuate, the individual must separate from the parent. Her formulation of the rapprochement subphase of the separation-individuation process is usefully applied to the termination of therapy. She explains how the toddler, excited about the newfound freedom to explore that comes with upright locomotion and a new level of cognitive development, first reaches out and explores the environment with great enthusiasm. Then, as if suddenly aware of the growing separation from mother, the toddler becomes very concerned about where mother is and how she is reacting to his or her explorations. The child experiences separation anxiety. If the mother responds by encouraging the child to explore and to conquer new challenges, the child transcends the anxiety and explores further. If the mother becomes depressed that the child has left her lap, excessively anxious about dangers connected with the child's explorations, rageful when the child falls or makes a mess, or just plain inattentive, the child is left feeling conflicted about new adventures, growth, and independent strivings.

Here is a metaphor for the termination of analysis or therapy. The price of completing the tasks of therapy and "graduating" is that the client must give up regular contact with and dependency on the therapist. When the client's experience of separation-individuation as a toddler was traumatic, and conflicts or abandonment anxiety lingers, the trade-off can be less than appealing. Some clients worry that the therapist will be enraged, others are certain the therapist does not really care anyway. Some clients worry that they will fall flat on their face once separate from the therapist, and others that it is the therapist who will fall apart or sink into depression once they are gone.

Whatever the fantasy, the therapist must help the client identify it and work it through so that separations can be experienced in a healthier fashion and personal growth and independence do not provoke anxiety and conflicts. The therapist, during

the course of the therapy, slowly begins to ask the earliest others "to leave the room," so that the new other, the therapist,
and the client can converse, during the termination phase, about
how this new relationship might end on a more growthful note.

Sometimes therapy is interrupted for external reasons. These
include the therapist's plan to move out of the area or cease
practicing, the client's plan to move, the client's lack of financial
resources to continue in therapy, and so forth. In discussing Burt's
therapy later in this chapter, I will have an opportunity to say
something about the shortage of financial resources. Here I will
comment on the situation where the therapist is seeing a client
in a clinic setting, perhaps as part of a psychology internship or
psychiatry residency, and is about to complete a phase of training and leave the clinic. Eugene Pumpian-Mindlin (1958) makes
some helpful suggestions on the management of this situation.
Many supervisors suggest that in such a predicament, the ther-
apist-trainee should wait until a few months before the time when
the internship or residency is to end, and then announce his or
her imminent departure. The rationale is that this leaves enough
time to work through termination issues and does not create a
situation earlier in the therapeutic encounter where the client
might be hesitant to deepen the therapeutic relationship for fear
of eventual abandonment.

I disagree with this teaching. It seems to me the therapist
should assume the client knows more about his or her abandonment issues and separation anxieties than does the therapist.
And the client's judgment, however compromised by the emotional disorder, should dictate the level to which he or she will
permit the therapeutic relationship to deepen. If the client does
not want to share certain personal thoughts, the therapist must
respect the defense. If this is not always true with all clients, it
certainly is the case in the particular circumstance where the
therapist knows this therapy will end on a particular date. I believe, as a general rule, the therapist should tell the client from
the beginning of therapy all she or he knows about the limit to
the length of the therapy. Then the client can decide, given the
time limit, how much to disclose and how dependent to become. Thus, if a therapist commences a therapeutic encounter
in September and knows she or he will be leaving the clinic at

the end of the following June, I believe the therapist is obligated to share this knowledge with the client. Some clients know they cannot tolerate a close relationship that will end in nine months. Others agree to the time limit but then always consider the time constraint when trying to decide what to share with the therapist and what not to share.

There are times when the therapist decides to discontinue the therapy before the criteria for termination have been met, not because of external considerations but because the therapy seems hopelessly stuck. This is essentially what happened in Frank B.'s case (chapter 2). There, the transference was erotized to such an extent that the analysis had to be terminated. The problem might be that the transference is erotized or that the analysis or therapy becomes so gratifying, for itself, independent of any amelioration of the symptoms, that the client resists growth in order to remain in this gratifying encounter. The therapist's task, in either case, is to interpret defensive aspects of the erotic feelings or the gratification from therapy—for example, the client makes this into a romantic relationship in order to seduce the therapist, as she did her father, into adoring her and never wishing to leave her. Or, the male client who enjoys the therapeutic relationship more than its healing effects uses the therapeutic relationship to escape from anxieties connected with establishing close relationships outside the consulting room. The therapist must make a serious attempt to help the client work through whatever resistances are present, but if, after a certain time spent confronting and interpreting the resistance, the erotized or overly gratifying relationship remains unaltered, the therapy might have to be terminated for the simple reason that there is insufficient clinical benefit to justify the therapist's time and the client's money. After the therapist tells the client that the therapy is to be discontinued, the task during the termination phase will be to examine the client's reactions to the therapist's decision to terminate, to help the client cope with the loss, and to maximize the benefits of the therapy. (For a discussion of erotized transference and how it is managed, see Greenson, 1967, and Ticho, 1966. For a discussion of stalemates in treatment, see Kernberg, 1984, pp. 241–53.)

When the therapy does reach the point where the criteria for termination have been met, the therapist and client agree upon a date for their last session, and the termination phase begins. Once the date has been set, the client's issues about termination emerge with renewed intensity. Even though each client experiences the ending differently, there are some identifiable patterns. Elsewhere (Kupers, 1981, pp. 196–212) I enumerate three: the client who so deeply resents what he experiences as rejection or abandonment by the therapist at the time of termination that he attacks the work of the therapy and undoes or fails to make use of the gains of treatment; the client who becomes so anxious and feels so helpless whenever the therapist takes a vacation or mentions termination that a regression occurs and the dependency seems interminable; and the client who refuses to become dependent on the therapist in the first place, or denies the dependency that has developed, and is being truthful when, at the time of termination, she or he says, "It's OK I won't miss you." There are other patterns, and there are accompanying emotions. Roy Schafer (1973) writes:

> The potential for virtually every significant human emotion resides in the termination situation. . . . The ideal termination would explore all these emotions—for example, feelings of deprivation and longing, guilt and unworthiness, gratitude and envy, triumph and defeat, love and betrayal, disappointment and elation, rage and grief, from all levels of psychosexual and ego development—insofar as they were accessible and significant. (p. 146)

Whatever the particular pattern, the client experiences negative as well as positive feelings toward the therapist. And there are good and bad memories of the therapeutic encounter. Examples of good memories are the times the therapist was warm and understanding when the client was needy, or the times the therapist gave a helpful interpretation or piece of advice, or the times pleasant thoughts about a recent therapy session carried the client through a depressing period between sessions. The bad memories are of times the therapist seemed mean, unsympathetic, unhelpful, or rejecting. If the client denies the negative feelings, for instance, while idealizing the therapist, it is the therapist's task to help the client discover the negative feelings and tolerate a certain amount of ambivalence. Negative feelings tend to emerge, if they are not denied, when the therapist goes on vacation. They are often reawakened when the client realizes the therapy is about to terminate.

If the negative feelings do not surface during therapy, and especially during the termination phase, it is likely they will grow stronger after termination—the need to idealize the therapist or deny negative feelings lessens when the therapist is no longer around—and undermine the benefits of the therapy. Therefore, it is especially important for the therapist, during the termination phase, to help the client be in touch with negative feelings, particularly feelings of disappointment, so that the client can look at those feelings as well as the positive ones, and in the balance, decide that though there are the negative feelings, the therapy has accomplished a great deal. Myrna Holden (1983), in a study comparing the outcomes of brief therapies where the negative feelings are explored with otherwise comparable therapies where they are not, finds that the exploration of negative feelings toward the therapist markedly increases the likelihood that the gains from therapy will be significant and lasting.

If the therapy has gone well, when it is time to terminate the therapy the client is ready to mourn the real loss, carry the therapist inside as a benign internalized object, and continue with life in a new and healthier way. This is the ideal. In reality, it seldom goes so smoothly. I will present vignettes that illustrate a few of the many diverse paths the termination of therapy can take, beginning with the termination of Sandra's therapy.

Sandra's Termination

As I have already mentioned, Sandra's termination issue was expressed early in the therapy. She believed that by refusing to share with me the gains in her life from therapy, she would avoid termination. If she let me know how much better she was doing because of our work, I would turn around and say: "Fine, that means we've accomplished what we came together for, and now it is time to end our relationship." As usual, there was a large kernel of truth in Sandra's formulation. We would some day end the therapeutic relationship, and yes, that would be when she had gained enough from our encounter. But this particular issue created problems in her relationship with me—a window on problems in her relationships with others. I found my interactions with her frustrating and unrewarding. I never heard about the changes in her life outside the consulting room, and all I got was icy silence. In addition, she never expressed any appreciation for what I did, and there were times when I just knew my interpretations were correct and useful, but she said nothing.

Sandra was reproducing with me a conflictual interaction she had with her mother. Beyond that, she was missing an important point about termination. Yes, when our work was done, we would part. That is the nature of therapy. But by the time that occurred, Sandra would be different in important respects, and one of those differences would be that she would better be able to tolerate separation and loss. And she would be ready to halt therapy and move on in her life. We discussed her shortsightedness in this regard and the way her failure to share gains and gratitude with me stifled our interactions.

Inevitably such discussions get around to the question of who decides on the actual date of termination. Sandra's original formulation was based on the assumption that the decision was totally in my hands. I would assess her improvement and tell her when we would terminate. Therefore she believed her only option was to hide the improvements from me, or refuse to grow altogether. Once we agreed that she would have a lot to say about the actual date of termination, she was able to share with me some of the ways therapy was helping her in her life. And, at first very hesitantly, she was able to express some appreciation for my efforts, including my patience with her while she was so cold and withholding.

Some time later, Sandra began to feel she had benefited a great deal from therapy and might be ready to terminate. By this time, she was in a relationship with a man that seemed to have a great deal of potential, had collected a rather impressive network of women intimates, was enjoying her work much more than she had ever before, and felt much more spontaneous in all of her endeavors. I reminded her of the time she had thought she would never want to terminate, and we laughed very tentatively about the turnaround. After hearing all the ideas and fantasies she could produce on the subject of termination, I responded that yes, I thought this was a good time to talk seriously of termination. Sandra was relieved, beamed proudly, and said that meant I thought she had accomplished the tasks of therapy and was ready to graduate.

The following week, Sandra returned depressed, and said she felt rejected by me, that I was trying to get rid of her and make room for someone else in my practice. Obviously, we had touched on another layer of issues she had about separation, and would have to work through those issues before terminating. It was not until several months later that we could mutually agree to set a date for our final session, and that date was several more months down the line. By then, we had spent enough time talking about Sandra's mixed feelings about our parting that we could end by merely sharing with each other how sad we would both be about not meeting regularly anymore.

Burt

Burt, by thirty-five, had done well in business. He was a vice-president in a small but profitable corporation. Then the floor caved in. The corporation was bought by a larger corporation, the larger corporation replaced the top administration with appointments of their own, and Burt was offered a lower-paying job with less status. Rather than accept this humiliating demotion, he decided to quit. He cashed in the stock options he had been accumulating as a manager in the corporation, the equivalent of about eight months' salary. He thought this would be plenty of time to find an even better position as a manager. But when six months passed and he found no work that he felt was worthy of his talents, he became disheartened. He began to lose sleep worrying about finding work.

Meanwhile he stopped seeing his friends, in part because he felt embarrassed about being unemployed. A single man, he had prided himself on being a playboy, and enjoyed dating and sleeping with several women in any given week. But by the time six months of unemployment had passed, he discovered that he was occasionally impotent, and since he could not predict when it would be, he stopped dating entirely. To make matters worse, he had by this time lost so much confidence that he was presenting himself poorly at job interviews and felt pessimistic about finding work. He decided to seek help from a therapist for the first time in his life.

When Burt first entered my office, he seemed meek and depressed. He told of a family with high standards, his father being a successful, self-made businessman, his older brother an attorney, and his younger sister a physician. His two siblings had always done well in school, while Burt was unmotivated and received average grades. He was more of a "regular guy," winning several varsity letters in high school, and then joining a fraternity in college and living "a wild life of boozing and womanizing." His parents never really approved of his performance until he entered a corporation after his college graduation and quickly worked his way up the management ladder. His father, who had never graduated high school and had always been intimidated by people with advanced degrees, was particularly impressed with the fact that Burt had more income than either of his better-educated siblings. Obviously, the loss of his job was a huge blow to Burt's ego, and Burt's narcissistic personality made him quite vulnerable. The massive depression that followed immobilized him. Burt seems to have suffered a narcissistic injury (Goldberg, 1973).

I listened to Burt's complaints about the unfairness of the corporate merger, confronted him about his tendency to negate all he had accomplished in his life to date just because of this one setback, and talked with him about the pressures and high standards he, like his father, set for himself, and how unforgiving they both were. After a few sessions, his depression lightened.

We discovered a fantasy he had from an early age that, because of his innate talent and charisma, and in spite of performing poorly in school, he would one day finesse his way into a high-paying job and surpass all of those who had applied themselves more and had better credentials (this would include his siblings, of course). The flip side of this rather grandiose fantasy was that the others he surpassed would be envious and would one day plot to deprive him of his status and power. The aftermath of the corporate merger seemed to fulfill his worst fears, including the corollary that he really did not deserve to be successful, and once exposed, would fall all the way to the bottom of the heap. Of course, this fantasy prevented him from developing any realistic goals while searching for work. At this point in our discussion, he suddenly realized that the jobs he was applying for were well beyond his experience and capabilities and that he was not seriously pursuing the jobs that were roughly equivalent to the one he had lost. With that realization, he proceeded to apply for a series of jobs and was offered an acceptable one.

Meanwhile, there were parallels in his fantasies about women. To begin with, we talked about the possibility that he might permit himself to occasionally perform poorly in a sexual encounter without assuming he was a hopelessly impotent man. In fact, the one woman he showed the most interest in found him more lovable when he was vulnerable in that way. After several months of therapy, Burt found a satisfactory job and felt much better about himself.

At the beginning of one session he announced that it would be his last. He was in difficult financial straits and would not be able to continue paying for therapy. He told me that I had helped him quite a bit but that he was doing fine now. Besides, he felt I was mainly helpful for people in acute crisis. I am very supportive. But if he were to continue in therapy, he would want to find someone who was "more confrontative, more probing." I felt the wind go out of my sails. He was demeaning me and the work I do. Taking a minute to recover from *my* narcissistic injury, I began to explore in my own mind, and then with him, reasons he might have to demean me and my work.

First, we talked about finances. Yes, he was having some difficulty paying his bills, and therapy was expensive. I did not try to minimize the possibility that he might need to halt the therapy for financial reasons. I suggested that even though that might be the case, perhaps there were also other reasons for his wanting to terminate. In other words, in response to the question whether it was really financial considerations or resistance that motivated him to terminate, my response was that it might be not one or the other, but both. When therapists interpret clients' claims that they cannot afford further therapy entirely as resistance, the client is justified in believing the therapist to be unsympathetic toward the painful reality of his financial straits. Alternatively, when the therapist appreciates the financial consideration and suggests there might also be some hidden resistance, the client is more open to hearing the latter interpretation and might even then be able to find a way to continue in therapy. I suggested we momentarily postpone the discussion about finances and talk for a little while about other reasons he might have to terminate. Then, if finances were still the determining consideration, he could terminate with some better understanding of his feelings about therapy and about our relationship.

Burt admitted he felt some disappointment toward me and the limited results of our work together. He remembered liking my warm and comforting style at the beginning of therapy when he needed support. But then he began to feel that anyone who was as supportive as I was would not be able to challenge him enough to get beyond his defenses and manipulations. I acknowledged that I had been supportive in the beginning, and conceded that perhaps I failed to confront him sufficiently at one point. Then I pointed out that I had in fact altered my approach with him in the three most recent sessions, but that each time I made an interpretation he minimized it, either saying he already knew that or denying he felt the way I assumed he was feeling. He thought about this, agreed that he had been defensive and that, in fact, the interpretations I was referring to had been both accurate and helpful. But after denying them, he had been too embarrassed to return and tell me how helpful they turned out to be.

He also revealed that he tended to think less of me when I accepted his criticism and changed my approach accordingly. We were then able to unravel a link to his disappointment in his father. Though his father was a successful businessman, he tended to be passive at home, permitting his wife to run the household and permitting his children to manipulate him and get away with lying. We discussed the difference between my changing my approach in response to his feedback about what is effective and what is ineffective, and whether or not this is necessarily a sign of weakness on my part. In fact, he had often wished that his father, instead of becoming critical when confronted about something, had been more responsive to his wishes.

This led us to the link between his need to devalue me and the termination issue. If he could devalue me sufficiently, he would not suffer much loss when we stop meeting. After all, if he did not derive much benefit from seeing me, then why should he feel anything about leaving me? His response to this interpretation was strong. He cried. He talked for a while about how much he had always longed to have a "heart-to-heart talk" with his father, and how impossible that was. His father could not even look him in the eye. Then he was able to see that his need to terminate therapy so precipitously was a way to avoid feelings of disappointment in me that would certainly arise if he continued to see me beyond the time when he was needy. He turned the conversation back to the question of finances and decided he could find some more money for therapy if he tried. We agreed to extend the time he had in mind for the termination phase of therapy—he had been thinking of ending after the day's session—and during the two-month time we agreed upon he was able to stay in touch with the grief he felt about terminating.

Janice

Janice, at thirty-four, had never been in a long-term relationship and had never held a job for more than a year or two. She began therapy by telling me how rotten all her lovers and bosses had been to her. Tired of complaining about all of them, she settled down, seemed almost to breathe a sigh of relief, and then changed the subject to depression. She was feeling bad about herself, wondering if it was really she, and not the lovers and the bosses, who was difficult to get along with and not very likeable. She cried, "I just get so lonely, sometimes I wonder if it's all worth it. Maybe I'd be better off dead."

After we talked long enough about whether or not suicide was a real danger, and Janice was able to assure both of us that it was not, she moved on to another important topic. She wanted more than anything to have a child. But she could not seem to stay in a relationship with a man long enough to accomplish that. She thought this was the main reason for her depression. She wondered, since all of her bosses were men, if the real difficulty might not be about relating to men. She had stayed away from men since the last man she saw—for two months—left her in a particularly brutal way six months before she commenced therapy. After several months of therapy, she began to feel better about men and decided to go out with a man her sister had been wanting to fix her up with.

She went out with the man. They slept together on the first date. Then he disappeared, failing to call and not returning the one phone call she nervously forced herself to make. She was more hurt than angry. During the next therapy session she cried. I made some brief statement I thought might be helpful—perhaps a lame attempt at an interpretation—and she pounced. Until this point in the therapy, it had seemed as if Janice could not stand to think of me as anything but the perfect therapist. She lauded my therapeutic skills as well as my caring manner, claiming I was very different than all those other unhelpful "shrinks" she had seen. Now, suddenly, I was not the caring, competent therapist. I was a "vindictive man who enjoys seeing patients suffer." She angrily berated me for my insensitivity, and added: "Besides, this therapy isn't helping me at all with my problems. My affair with this man was just as much a fiasco as all the rest."

In the midst of the ensuing discussion about what I was and was not doing for her, Janice complained that I was not taking care of her enough. I was not "hearing what hurts and doing something about it," and she thought it was because I did not really care about her. The particular statements of mine she found unhelpful and objectionable were the ones where I interpreted or confronted her about something she was doing rather than sympathized with her about the pain she was feeling. Thus, she found my questions—for instance, if she might not have waited longer to sleep with that man—to be very insensitive and uncaring.

Janice was expressing her belief that therapy is a place where the client is taken care of, where the therapist practically always satisfies the client's needs, within reason of course. At some point in our discussion, I made it clear that I do not see therapy quite that way. Of course there is a caring relationship wherein the work of therapy is done. But that work does not only, or even mainly, include support and caretaking. The therapist must confront the client at times and interpret what lies beneath the surface, and the interpretations might cause a certain amount of pain, or at least not be what the client would like to hear. I suggested that she might be angry about my doing that, precisely because her fantasy is that I will take care of her and never introduce any anxiety or tension into our relationship. But, I pointed out, my interventions are aimed at accomplishing the work of therapy, and I plan to make more like them. When I acknowledged that this might make her angry and mentioned that it takes a certain amount of courage for her to share with me that she is angry, she relaxed a little and admitted she sometimes just feels like having me take care of her, even though she knows that is not necessarily the best use of therapy.

This kind of exchange had to be repeated many times during the course of therapy with Janice. For instance, one time she was angry at me because she had called me the evening before and I did not answer her message until the following morning. We talked about her feeling disappointed. I acknowledged that some of her disappointment was warranted—I might have answered her message the night before and saved her a certain amount of anguish. But she would not let the subject go. She kept returning to the fact that I did not answer her message. At some time during the session I repeated my speech about the difference between her view of therapy and mine, and added that the places where disappointments and betrayals occur in the therapeutic relationship are often the best places to do some work on the difficulty she was having with men—that is, here was an opportunity to examine in more depth this therapeutic relationship with a man.

Of course, Janice was one of the clients I dreaded telling of my upcoming vacations. She typically became angry, complained I was leaving her just when she needed me most, and either missed the session before I was to leave, or complained for several sessions after I returned about how hard her life had been in the interim. Repeatedly, I acknowledged her anger, pointed out the pattern in her reactions to disappointments and separations, and linked the whole issue to her constant fear while growing up of abandonment by her mother. Her mother was severely depressed and inattentive most of the time, and had been hospitalized for depression for two months when Janice was a year and a half old. In whatever words made sense at the time, and with reference to whatever hardships in her life she felt I abandoned her to, I repeatedly attempted to distinguish between our separation—an unavoidable facet of any relationship—and abandonment. The abandoner is by definition inattentive to the needs of the abandoned one—as her mother very definitely was at the time she was hospitalized—while the periodic separations that occur in any relationship are not necessarily due to insensitivity on the part of the one who leaves, and can be less traumatic when the two people discuss the scheduled break in advance and process some of the feelings involved. Thus, even though I unilaterally planned my vacations, and she did not have the power to prevent me from going, I did take care to inform her about it, assured her I would be back on a specified date, and then paid attention to her feelings and concerns about our separation. This kind of exchange occurred with each of my vacations, and gradually Janice learned that separations do not necessarily represent abandonments.

Even though this general discussion occurred repeatedly during the course of Janice's long and difficult therapy, Janice felt betrayed and abandoned anew when termination time neared. Any time I even mentioned the subject, Janice would become enraged, claiming I could not wait to get rid of her. She believed I would use her two hours a week to see a woman I preferred: "a prettier one, one who is easier to get along with and is more in awe of you."

After several such exchanges, when therapy had proceeded for three years and Janice seemed to be doing very well, I again broached the subject of termination, this time in the context of reviewing Janice's impressive progress in therapy. She still was not in a long-term relationship with a man, but she was dating and optimistic about finding Mr. Right someday. And though she still became angry when I announced a missed session or a vacation, the anger was not as intense, she could talk about it rather than screaming or acting out, and she could let go of the subject after a brief discussion. She had decided somewhere toward the middle of therapy to enter graduate school and pursue a profession—an objective she was well on the way to accomplishing. And she had for some time been complaining about a lack of funds to continue therapy. Even though the time seemed right for a serious discussion of termination, she exploded more forcefully than I had seen for many months and renewed her accusations that I was just trying to get rid of her because I preferred to spend the hours seeing someone else.

When I raised the question of termination once again with Janice, she admitted that one of the reasons she did not want to talk about it was that she could not imagine my being absent from her life. She shared a fantasy she had that after therapy was completed, we might become lovers. Barring that, she would at least like to be good friends. The discussion turned to the different types of relationships two individuals might have and the choices that are made along the way. She had once told me about her ambivalence about sleeping with a close male friend of hers, how she feared the romantic relationship would not work out and then she would be losing her only close friendship with a man. I reminded her of that discussion and focused for a moment on the choice she had. Therapy involved a comparable choice. For the therapy to be effective, there must be a certain therapeutic distance in the consulting room. After all, no one wanted to be in therapy with a relative, a lover, or a friend. She agreed: "Of course not, you need more objectivity than that." I took advantage of the moment to point out the choice one makes when one enters a therapeutic encounter. Though the client might have conflicts about giving up the possibility of a different kind of relationship with the therapist—as friend or lover, for instance—there is the choice to designate this person as one's therapist. Even if attractions and romantic fantasies crop up during the course of the therapy, the choice is binding. In any case, much can be gained from a therapeutic relationship, making giving up the alternatives worthwhile. (This is an oversimplified synopsis of a discussion that occupied three sessions and was punctuated with awkward silences, tears, and occasional outbursts of anger and resentment.)

Janice eventually agreed the time for termination was near. She and I spent several months—probably the larger part of the termination phase of her therapy—talking about the difference between a termination of therapy that is agreed upon by both partners, and abandonment, that happens when one person unilaterally leaves and the other person is not near ready to carry on by herself. Her affect during the first half of the termination phase was typically anger, and during the second half sadness. Remember, Janice's early idealization of me was a defensive attempt to avoid negative feelings. Only later, after I disappointed her by not being as sensitive as she would have liked when she felt abandoned by a man, did the negativity surface. Recall the general principle: if the negative transference is not brought to the surface and sufficiently worked through, the client is left alone after termination with a stockpile of unarticulated or unconscious bad feelings that will ultimately undermine the gains of the therapy. But if the negative feelings can be worked through, they can be seen in perspective with the positive feelings, and the latter can be preserved in lasting change. Eventually Janice was able to integrate the two, telling me at one point that she was finally able to see what I meant when I said a person could be angry at someone close, express it, and still appreciate the value of the relationship and mourn the loss.

The ending is not always as ideal as it turned out in Janice's case. For some people, the trauma of parting looms larger than any gain they can imagine getting from the therapeutic encounter. Consider for a moment the hospitalized psychotic patient who seems to do very well on the inpatient unit, quickly responds to medications and milieu therapy so that the hallucinations and bizarre behaviors that landed him in the hospital are under control, is a work leader in daily group-therapy sessions, is very attached to one of the staff who meets regularly with him, and seems motivated to make plans to live independently. Then his primary therapist arranges a job interview for him as part of discharge planning. The night before the interview, the psychotic symptoms suddenly reappear. The patient becomes violent and uncontrollable to the extent that he must be isolated in a security room and have his medication dosages raised. What happened? It seems the prospect of leaving the by now familiar and safe ward and its staff is more frightening than the prospect of holding a job and being independent is attractive. This, in a nutshell, is the dilemma of many people whose emotional symptomatology is less severe and who never need hospitalization. But their intense dread of partings causes their therapies to mis-fire. Janice and I were able to work through this issue. Many therapies fail because it is too deep an issue for the client to transcend.

As therapists take on more difficult cases, such as those in-volving primitive character disorders, the termination issue looms even larger in the consulting room. And consequently, new strategies must be devised to treat clients for whom the trauma of termination seems to outweigh the potential benefits of en-tering into a therapeutic relationship. More attention must be given to termination issues, even early in therapy when pre-cursors of the termination issue surface. Then, like psychoanal-ysis, psychotherapy with less disturbed clients follows the same path, deeper-lying recesses of the psyche are explored, and as a consequence termination is considered a more important issue to focus on. I will conclude this chapter on the termination of long-term psychotherapy with a discussion of the countertrans-ference.

Countertransference

In chapter 1 I mentioned Freud's fear of dependency—his own and others'—and speculated that might be the reason he failed at the time of termination to work through with analysands their dependency on him. Since Freud, therapists have paid more attention to their clients' feelings about ending the therapeutic relationship. Longer therapies that probe for deeper-lying con-flicts tend to foster more dependency, resulting in heightened termination issues, and consequently the modern therapist can-not minimize the client's feelings of loss as Freud attempted to do with the Wolfman.

Therapists have issues about termination, too. Laplanche and Pontalis (1973) define countertransference as "the whole of the analyst's unconscious reactions to the individual analysand—es-pecially to the analysand's own transference" (p. 92). I am using a broader definition, including conscious as well as unconscious reactions. Some of the therapist's reactions are blatantly inap-propriate, for instance, concern that when this client terminates the therapist will have difficulty filling the vacant time slot. In practice, concerns like this probably account for many overly lengthy therapies. The therapist, out of self-interest, colludes with the client's dependency and prolongs the therapy. Other sentiments are more honorable, but still must be suppressed or worked through privately by the therapist. For instance, the therapist might realize that he or she is overly identified with a particular client, very fond of the client, or even secretly in love with the client, and will have great difficulty saying goodbye. Weddington and Cavenar (1979) suggest that the dearth of clinical literature on termination reflects the fact that therapists have difficulty coping with their countertransference feelings.

In relation to these very human feelings, the basic rule of psychotherapy, as of analysis, is that the therapist must keep a running account of the countertransference, attempt to understand the interface and crossings of transference and countertransference, utilize countertransference feelings to inform interpretations where appropriate—for instance, if there is reason to believe the therapist's feelings toward the client result from the client's projections or projective indentifications—and then work through the other countertransference feelings and issues privately in order not to burden the client with them and not to let them interfere with the progress of the therapy. Some therapists, for instance, have a need to foster dependency in their clients, or to collude with their clients' dependency needs, and if their countertransference is not worked through, therapies they conduct become ineffective and interminable.

One particular countertransference theme often emerges at termination and deserves mention. The therapist's task is to help the client transcend psychological constrictions and grow. When all goes well, there is gratification in the work, gratification that resembles the parent's when the child grows and flourishes. As the time for termination nears, the therapist, depending on what unconscious conflicts and fantasies there are about separation and loss, might experience some difficulty letting go of the client, just as the parent might when the child is ready to leave home.

David Malan (1973) describes the "social-worker syndrome" that is present for many therapists. The social worker takes care of clients better than she or he was taken care of as a child and vicariously identifies with the client who is receiving such good care. But then the social worker (or therapist, to the degree the syndrome is present) resents the client who is receiving such good care, care the social worker would like to have received him- or herself.

To the extent this syndrome is present in the therapist, there is a problem at the time of termination. The therapist derives a certain amount of gratification from the client's growth and success. As long as the therapeutic relationship continues, all is well. Then, when it is time for therapist and client to part, the therapist might feel some resentment that the client has benefited from the therapist's best efforts, and then is going to leave, and will likely forget about the therapist soon thereafter. After all, the child remains connected with the parent after leaving home, but the termination of therapy is usually more final. Sometimes a client's idiosyncratic defensive maneuvers at the time of termination aggravate the therapist's countertransference feelings. This happens, for instance, when the client attempts to minimize feelings of loss by not recognizing and appreciating how much the therapist has helped. Ideally, of course, the therapist has worked through in a personal analysis or therapy the inner conflicts that lead to this kind of resentment.

Sandra's tendency to devalue the therapeutic relationship certainly brought out the social-worker syndrome in me. As the time of termination neared, she reactivated a defense mechanism I had interpreted earlier in our work together. She stopped telling me about the positive things going on in her life outside the consulting room and told me only about her problems. At the same time, she expressed no appreciation for anything we had accomplished in therapy, and even began telling me about a friend—remember, it was only as a result of our work that she would risk close friendship—who was able to enter a relationship with a man and become pregnant before terminating therapy. For awhile, during the termination phase, our meetings were tense. I found myself confronting her on details—she would arrive a few minutes late, or fail to tell me a dream until two weeks later—but there was a bitter edge to my interpretations of her resistance. Sandra was of course trying to diminish her feelings of loss by devaluing me, and perhaps her unconscious fantasy was that if I was angry at her for her lack of appreciation, and retaliated with insensitivity and meanness (as either of her parents would have done), the parting would be angry, but easier. Eventually, I discovered the way her devaluing enraged the frustrated social worker in me, and I was able to put this into proper perspective with the loss I was feeling as termination neared. Only then could I point out, with the correct timing and dosage and without the bitter edge, that she was defensively minimizing the benefits of our work together in order to make the parting easier. She agreed, and her tears confirmed that we had successfully worked through an important part of the termination process.

There are as many countertransference themes at termination as there are transference themes. For instance, Martin and Schurtman (1985) discuss the therapist's feelings about loss of the professional role that had differentiated therapist from client during the course of the therapy—that is, when the transference is resolved, the therapist is no longer idealized, and the two are more alike than different in the mourning they experience at their parting. Again, as David Cooper (1970) writes: "The guarantee of good therapy is that the therapist is familiar enough with the machinations of his internal family and has them well enough tamed" (p. 5).

Chapter 4

The Clinical Logic
of Termination

THIS DISCUSSION has so far remained on the clinical level, but a premise that underlies this work is that the clinical and social levels must be integrated if we are to understand the meaning of termination. This chapter will serve as the transition from the purely clinical discussion to one that integrates the clinical and the social levels. The concept of a clinical logic touches on both.

What do I mean by clinical logic? The term does not refer to particular psychodynamic or metapsychological formulations, or even particular theoretical stances. Rather, the clinical logic becomes apparent only from a historical vantage point, from which it is possible to view a pattern that is repeated with each of the major innovations that have shaken the field of psychoanalysis and psychotherapy since Freud. The pattern goes something like this: (1) Clinicians, often because they are examining a new clientele, or seeing a familiar clientele for new reasons, hear a new set of complaints or symptoms. (2) The new list of symptoms is related to new or revised diagnoses. (3) New theory is generated to explain etiology and guide treatment. (4) New therapeutic techniques are devised. (5) The criteria for termination and the management of the termination phase of therapy are altered accordingly. (6) It is argued that the technique and the approach to termination are now the specific indicated treatment for this particular diagnostic category.

How does this clinical logic touch on both the clinical and social levels? The logic is clearly reflected in the clinical literature, as I will illustrate with the work of Heinz Kohut. In terms of the social level, recall the line Freud (Freud and Breuer,

1895, p. 305) drew between "neurotic misery" and "common un-happiness," and my contention in the introduction that clinicians have been steadily moving that line, ceding to the realm of neurotic misery (or newer varieties of psychopathology) much of what once might have been considered part of everyday unhappiness. The movement of that line is a social phenomenon, even if clinicians believe it is merely a matter of their capability to treat more symptoms with their greater understanding of psychopathology and more advanced therapeutic techniques. There are social roots to developments in the field of psychoanalysis and psychotherapy, and social implications to the widespread practice of therapy. Indeed, the clinical logic of termination is the mechanism whereby the line is moved. I will discuss the clinical logic in this chapter; in chapter 5 I will examine a contradiction inherent in the logic regarding the assignment of clients to brief or long-term therapy; and in chapter 7 I will explain how the clinical logic serves as the mechanism for larger social developments.

At this writing, a debate is raging at the national level of the American Psychiatric Association: Should the APA endorse the report of its Task Force on Treatments of Psychiatric Disorders, which "develops treatment principles for major diagnoses, discusses areas of agreement and controversy, and discusses the goals as well as pros and cons of various modalities in treating patients with these disorders?" (APA, 1987a). The pros of endorsing the treatment manual are that naming indicated treatments, such as brief therapy for posttraumatic stress disorders, medications or cognitive therapy for depression, behavior modification for phobias, or long-term supportive psychotherapy for borderline character, would permit more objective peer review and effective allocation of treatment resources. The cons touch on the same points: insurance companies will deny payment for treatments not indicated in the manual, thus undermining the clinician's judgment in each case, and patients' attorneys will cite the manual in malpractice suits. Whatever the outcome of the debate, the point is that the clinical logic leads to the idea of a manual that designates specific treatments for each of a growing list of emotional disorders.

I will discuss each of the six steps of this clinical logic. I could use any of the major turnings in therapeutic approach that have occurred since Freud. For instance, Wilhelm Reich (1933) expanded the expectations as well as the number of potential candidates for psychoanalysis by suggesting, in direct contradiction to Freud's early view that the analyst cures only the neurosis and leaves the analysand with the same underlying character structure, that character can be changed by analysis. What would be required, of course, would be a deeper analysis, one that would get to the core of the "character armor." Since Reich, analysts have been analyzing clients with ever more serious character disorders, and the analyses have grown longer in the process.

Or I could use Melanie Klein's innovations in theory and technique to illustrate the logic of termination. Where Freud would not treat psychotics because he felt their extreme narcissism made it impossible for them to direct enough energy toward the treating analyst to make the transference analyzable, Klein (1948) treated psychotic patients and created new theory in the process. In doing so, she moved the prototype for therapy back from the oedipal stage of development to the earliest infant-mother relationship and searched for infantile defense mechanisms in the transference relationship. Her position that the conflicts of the early months of life must be analyzed before termination could be considered also resulted in longer analyses.

Heinz Kohut's self psychology, a more recent innovation that has received attention among therapists, also illustrates the logic of termination. In what follows, I will explain Kohut's theory in greater detail than any of the others. This is not to say that I think Kohut and his followers have found the single correct way to practice therapy. But his ideas are very helpful, and his formulation about termination happens to illustrate the clinical logic very nicely. Therefore, as I list and comment upon the six steps of the clinical logic, I will explicate just enough of Kohut's theory to illustrate each point.

1. *Clinicians hear from clients about a new set of symptoms.* In Freud's day it was likely a paralyzed limb, a debilitating obsession, or an inability to get out of bed that brought someone to see a psychoanalyst. Today, therapists' practices take them to

more varied settings: the schools, courts, prisons, and work-places. Every time they enter a new situation they hear different sets of complaints: about learning disabilities, disruptive behaviors, violence, or work disabilities. And in their private practices, therapists frequently see clients who are highly functional people who are just not happy with their lives. At the same time, therapists are seeing more severely disturbed people than did early analysts. In those days, people with severe character disorders would have been considered poor candidates for treatment. With all these changes, the list of complaints therapists hear and aim to treat grows ever longer. For instance, in the private consulting room, with more people choosing to undergo therapy for relatively subtle problems, the therapist hears a lot about troubled intimacies, inability to be creative, feelings of inner emptiness, and so forth. The new symptoms Reich heard about involved rigidity of character, while Melanie Klein heard about severe mood swings and attacks of mania or paranoia.

For Kohut, the new list includes more subtle hindrances to intimacy and creativity. He realizes that many of his analysands are undergoing psychoanalysis for reasons directly related to their narcissistic personalities. Many demonstrate the narcissist's self-centeredness, tendency to exploit others, insensitivity to others' needs and feelings, addictive patterns, need for sexual conquests to bolster self-esteem, and/or rageful response when others criticize or refuse their demands. But he thinks the narcissist's bravado is merely a cover for another, possibly more significant list of symptoms: low self-esteem, depression, feelings of inner emptiness, hypersensitivity to slights, a lack of vitality and creativity, loneliness, experiencing repeated failure in their relationships, preoccupations with bodily or psychosomatic complaints, and a recurring feeling of fragmentation.

Once he found this list of depth symptomatology in his narcissistic patients, Kohut began to discover that other patients, many of whom did not come to treatment with the typical outward appearance of the narcissistic personality, also complained of these same symptoms. Kohut's discussion turns to the narcissistic traits we all might have: there's a narcissist in many of us, even in those of us whose problem seems the opposite of narcissism, that is, an inability to muster enough of the the aforementioned bravado to be self-assertive.

2. *The new list of symptoms is related to a new or revised diagnosis.* As therapists leave the private consulting room to venture into schools, prisons, and other settings, they hear new lists of complaints from the clients they encounter there, and begin to create new diagnostic categories. They diagnose hyperkinesis or attention-deficit disorder in the schools, impulsive dyscontrol syndrome or conduct disorder in the prisons, and work inhibition in the workplace.

Meanwhile, in the private consulting room, clients are always bringing in new lists of complaints, and therapists inventing new diagnoses. Therapists rarely examine someone and conclude there is no identifiable psychopathology. There is always a bit of neurosis, a character disorder, or, in the most current psychological terms, a borderline or psychotic core lying somewhere deep inside even the most sane-appearing individual.

For instance, where once the women seen by analysts were likely to be housewives or not working, today's therapist sees many successful professional women. As these women complain of insecurity, fears that they are just fooling someone about their competence and will soon be found out, and ambivalence about the pressures of work life, a new diagnostic category is invented: "the impostor complex in high achieving women" (Clance and Imes, 1978).

There are official diagnoses, and there are unofficial ones. The impostor complex is still unofficial, as is the midlife crisis (Jaques, 1965). The official list grows; each successive edition of the *Diagnostic and Statistical Manual* (APA, 1980, 1987b) lists many more categories than did the previous one. And some of what were unofficial diagnoses become official. Thus, posttraumatic stress disorder and panic attack made it into the last revision, amid much publicity, and accompanied by conferences and continuing education courses for therapists on how to diagnose and treat these newer conditions. Other unofficial diagnoses, even ones as well known and widely applied as the "as-if personality" (Deutsch, 1942), never make it onto the official list. Whether

the diagnosis makes the official list or not, this step in the clinical logic is the same: new symptom lists are linked with new
diagnostic categories.

Reich's new diagnoses included the character disorders, especially the obsessional, masochistic, hysterical, and narcissistic
characters. The diagnoses that interested Klein were manic-de-
pressive psychosis, schizophrenia, and the less severe but still
problematic schizoid personality. W. R. D. Fairbairn (1941) and
D. W. Winnicott (1965) made the last category a very familiar
one in clinical settings.

Kohut's new diagnostic category is the disorder of the self.
And Kohut's work nicely illustrates this step of the logic at work
in the private consulting room. Narcissism is not a new diagnosis. Freud considered infantile narcissism a normal developmental stage and felt the psychotic was essentially regressing to
that level. Lou Andreas-Salomé (1962) pointed out the link between narcissism and creativity, and she cautioned that by too
quickly pathologizing narcissism, analysts risked jettisoning artistic creativity in their construction of the "normal" personality.
For a long time, analysts employed the diagnosis "narcissistic
personality," but felt that psychoanalysis with these patients was
not indicated or not likely to be fruitful. Then in the late 1960s
and early 1970s, largely because of the work of Kohut (1971) and
Otto Kernberg (1975), clinicians began to feel they finally understood narcissism well enough to offer effective psychotherapy.

While the narcissistic personality is not a new diagnosis, Kohut
employs a diagnosis that is new, the disorder of the self. For
Kohut, the self is both a psychic structure, "the center of the
individual's psychological universe" (1977, p. 311), and the subject (the "I") who experiences and acts. Thus, frailty or fragmentation of the self results in a lack of cohesion and continuity
of experience, problems with self-esteem, and a feeling of emptiness and lack of agency in one's life. This is the narcissist's
dilemma. Kohut sees an unstable and very vulnerable self beneath the surface bluster of the narcissistic personality.

Once he has uncovered a structural disorder of the self at the
core of the narcissistic personality, Kohut proceeds to identify
the same kind of structural defect in analysands who would be

less likely diagnosed narcissists on the basis of their surface appearance. Some people, for instance, suffer from "insufficient narcissistic libido," and their muted, attention-avoiding presentation and sense of themselves as boring is quite the opposite of the stereotypic narcissist's attention grabbing. Yet they suffer from the same kind of underlying disorder of the self.

Kohut sets up a spectrum of disorders of the self. At the most pathological end, the psychotic is someone with an extensively damaged, noncohesive self. The borderline states are slightly less damaged. According to Kohut (Kohut and Wolf, 1978): "Here the break-up, the enfeeblement, or the functional chaos of the nuclear self are also permanent or protracted, but, in contrast to the psychoses, the experiential and behavioral manifestations of the central defect are covered by complex defences" (p. 415). Then, the spectrum includes the narcissistic personality disorders per se. Finally, there are the narcissistic traits, or "character types in the narcissistic realm frequently encountered in everyday life and they should, in general, not be considered as forms of psychopathology but rather as variants of the normal human personality with its assets and defects" (p. 422).

In other words, Kohut has reorganized all the diagnostic cubbyholes in order to make room for a category of psychopathology he invented, the disorder of the self. He is not the first to reformulate the diagnostic nomenclature on the basis of an innovative diagnosis. W. R. D. Fairbairn (1941) did the same, explaining the differences among paranoia, hysteria, and obsessional neurosis with reference to the different ways patients employ schizoid mechanisms. And Masterson (1976) tends to do the same thing, though not as explicitly. The borderline character diagnosis was once employed only in regard to patients whose lifestyle and capacity for reality testing were both so marginal that they seemed literally on the border between neurosis and psychosis. But Masterson diagnoses the borderline character in a broad spectrum of people: in successful professional people with families, whom he identifies as "better adjusted borderlines" with a neurotic presentation, as well as in lower-level borderlines who appear almost psychotic. Where Fairbairn finds schizoid mechanisms in many different diagnostic categories and Masterson finds borderline psychopathology, Kohut finds disorders of the self. Each then goes to offer a theoretical formulation about the diagnostic typology he has created.

3. *New theory is generated to explain etiology and guide treatment.* A wonderful thing about psychoanalytic theory is its constant evolution. When analysts encounter new problems, they first attempt to adapt old theories to explain the new findings. Eventually an innovator comes along and reformulates the whole theory to include, often to highlight, the new problems; there is a shift in paradigm (Kuhn, 1962). All the major schools of psychoanalytic thought began this way. Reich (1933) theorized the early development of character styles, how they are lastingly preserved in character structure, and the defensive functions of character. When the new findings are psychotic phenomena, the theory shifts the prototype to the infantile stage and stresses more primitive defense mechanisms. This is where Melanie Klein (1948), W. R. D. Fairbairn (1941), and D. W. Winnicott (1965) offer theoretical breakthroughs.

When the new findings are subtle kinds of dysphoria in relatively high-functioning individuals, the theory focuses on nuances of the transference that were previously considered inconsequential. Kohut's theory is an example. He begins with an empirical observation: in analysis, clients with a narcissistic personality tend to be very attuned to the analyst's degree of empathy. He notices that when the analyst fails to empathize the analysand becomes depressed, rageful, or merely more lifeless. Then he identifies two kinds of transferences that typically evolve: the idealizing transference and the mirror transference. (He would later add the alter-ego transference where the analysand seeks sameness with the analyst [Kohut and Wolf, 1978]. In the former, the analysand idealizes the therapist and then feels powerful because she or he is connected with such a powerful person. Or; in the latter, the analysand uses the analyst as a mirror, demanding the analyst's attention and praise and becoming angry or depressed when it is not forthcoming. Whether an idealizing or a mirror transference evolves, the clients seem very vulnerable to criticism and slights and have trouble remembering that they are worthwhile individuals.

Kohut theorizes that these transferences and the analysand's sensitivity to the analyst's failure to empathize represent the reactivation in the analytic situation of a conflictual phase of childhood, the period just after the one Freud termed infantile narcissism. During this phase, the child is supposedly no longer merged with an all-powerful parent and no longer feels the bliss of that narcissistic merger, but also is very hesitant to give it up. Psychologically speaking, one strategy available to the child is to idealize the parent, who by now is viewed as somewhat separate, and then: "Since all bliss and power now reside in the idealized object, the child feels empty and powerless when he is separated from it and he attempts, therefore, to maintain a continuous union with it" (Kohut, 1971, p. 37). The child, grown into the narcissistic adult, attempts that kind of union once more with the idealized analyst. Another strategy for the child is to retain from the narcissistic phase a grandiose self and to demand from others recognition of that grandiosity—that is, to use others as a mirror of the self's greatness. These two childish strategies are what the narcissist reenacts with the analyst as the idealizing and mirror transferences.

Why do some people develop narcissistic personalities while others do not? Kohut's answer is that pathological narcissism (that connected with a disorder of the self) results from a parental failure to empathize, and that earlier and more extensive or traumatic failures result in more severe disorders, the worst being psychosis. In the normal case, there is a narcissistic stage of development, just as Freud said. The child does have a difficult time giving up the feelings of oneness, power, and bliss that are part of that stage. But the parents' empathic responses permit the child to make the transition to greater autonomy.

Specifically, the parent first allows him- or herself to be used by the child as a "self-object." "The expected control over such [self-object] others is then closer to the concept of the control which a grownup expects to have over his own body and mind than to the concept of the control which he expects to have over others" (Kohut, 1971, p. 27). The "good enough" parent (Winnicott, 1965) first responds empathically to the child's need to control him or her as a self-object, and then, in a phase-appropriate way, gradually weans the child from this need for narcissistic control by disappointing the child in incremental steps that are more palatable to the child.

According to Kohut, in order to grow up with a healthy self, the individual must be sufficiently nourished in the narcissistic sector of the evolving personality. For instance, the very young child says a first word, takes a step, or sings a simple song, and the audience—parents and friends—claps. The child momentarily experiences being on center stage and enjoys the attention. Gradually the child learns she or he cannot remain always in the limelight. The teenager who sings a simple song and expects applause is courting serious disappointment or mockery. But the child who never has the experience of being thus on center stage grows up with "insufficient narcissistic libido" and experiences a lack of joy and a certain flatness to life.

In other words, the parent incrementally teaches the child that she or he cannot have constant attention and praise, but includes the message that the child is still talented and lovable enough, and will have attention and praise at least for certain moments here and there. It is parental empathy that guides the process and determines how big the steps of disillusionment can be without traumatizing the young and still very vulnerable child.

If this is done right, according to Kohut, there occurs a process he terms "transmuting internalization." By this Kohut means that the phase-appropriate disappointments in important others play a part in the formation of structures within the child's psyche—the precursors and building blocks of mature intrapsychic structures like the self and the ego—that permit the child to feel an inner source of strength, praiseworthiness, and vitality. The strength of the evolving self depends on the phase-appropriateness of the disappointments. Optimally, the child gives up its self-objects, its grandiosity, and its need for idealization, and in their place is constructed a self that permits autonomy, vitality, creativity, the capacity for an inner regulation of self-esteem as opposed to needing others' mirroring to feel good, and the capacity to be empathic toward others.

With this model of normal development, it is easy to see what goes wrong in the case of the narcissist. The disappointments are too large, occur before the child is able to tolerate them, or are not balanced with enough gratification to make them palatable. The parental failure of empathy is usually connected to the parents' own psychopathology—for instance, they are too narcissistic themselves to be capable of empathy, even for their children. Or events like the death of a parent might play a part, or some as yet poorly understood constitutional factor might be involved. But in any case, by extrapolating backward from the kinds of transferences Kohut observes with the adult narcissist, he develops a theory to explain the disorders of the self.

A clinical example: A young man came to see me in a panic about the breaking up of a three-year relationship with a woman he described as the most beautiful and exciting he had ever met. He was depressed. He had always wondered what she saw in him since she seemed to "have it all," and he felt quite dull and uninteresting in comparison. His mother was quite narcissistic, being a frustrated stage actress, quite dramatic and vain, and was interested mainly in the status of the men she (a divorcée) could attract. My client learned very early in life that his best chance of feeling close to his mother would occur when she seemed depressed and he went to her and comforted her by saying something about how pretty she looked. In other words, there was no way for him to get her to pay attention to what was going on in his life independent of her.

In the first few therapy sessions, he had trouble finding material to talk about. He would start to talk about something and then stop and say it really was not worth saying much about. He was afraid he was boring me. We were able to link this fear to his tendency to attribute all excitement to his woman friend and to worry that he was boring in comparison, and his correct assumption as a youngster that his mother found her own problems much more interesting than his. By focusing attention on this theme while at the same time insisting I wanted to hear just what was on his mind, I was able to encourage him to talk a little longer about one issue and then another. Minutes later he brightened up and became enthusiastic as he told me about an essay he was in the midst of writing.

4. *New therapeutic techniques are devised.* I outlined in chapter 2 some developments in the field of psychoanalysis. Therapies tend to grow longer, delve more deeply into the psyche,

use earlier phases of childhood as a prototype for the psycho-pathology as well as the transference, and focus on more primitive defense mechanisms. This is one major trend. Another is for therapists to claim more for their techniques and to begin to intensify the therapeutic onslaught so that certain conditions can be treated in a very short time. As I will explain in some detail in chapter 5, the advent of brief therapy also fits the logic of termination very nicely. Where the innovations of Reich, Klein, and Kohut result in a lengthening and deepening of the therapeutic venture, the brief therapists concentrate on more circumscribed symptoms and prescribe a more abbreviated treatment. Characteristic of both the trend toward lengthier and the trend toward briefer therapy is that therapeutic techniques are altered to fit newly discovered syndromes and diagnostic categories.

This makes sense. Why should therapists manage every treatment in the same way, always "peeling away each layer of the onion" as if they did not know, in line with their diagnostic impressions, what issues to expect and in what order? Generally, treatment strategies proliferate because clinicians gain experience with various emotional conditions and then feel they can better aim their interventions at the heart of the matter in ensuing treatments of like diagnosed individuals.

Continuing with the theories I have mentioned, Reich advises constant confrontation of the habitual patterns of defense—for instance, the idiosyncratic tone of voice or posturing that the client displays in the consulting room—that are typical of each character type; Klein advises early and constant interpretation of the earliest infantile conflicts, especially as they become reenacted in the transference; and Kohut stresses the therapeutic uses of empathy.

Again, I will explain Kohut's emphasis in a little greater detail. Kohut has shifted the attention of followers from the classical analytic theory of unconscious conflicts and disavowed wishes to the ways patients with disorders of the self attempt, through their narcissistic symptoms, to restore cohesion and vitality to their lives while actually experiencing deadness inside. Therefore his treatment strategy focuses on how the therapist might have to temporarily serve as a self-object to help the client get past that fixation and attain healthy relationships.

He does not attempt to interpret symptoms in relation to the unconscious drives they symbolize. Rather, he allows the narcissistic transference, be it idealizing or mirroring, to evolve in the consulting room. The therapist must be empathic to accomplish this: "For long periods the analyst must participate empathically in the psychic imbalance from which the patient suffers; he must show understanding for the patient's painful embarassment and for his anger that the act that has been committed cannot be undone. Then, gradually, the dynamics of the situation can be approached" (Kohut, 1971, p. 231). Kohut stresses that this does not mean gratifying the client's needs, except the need to be accurately and empathically understood (Baker and Baker, 1987). Rather, the therapist allows the narcissistic transference to develop and then helps the client understand that there are ways she or he uses the therapist as a self-object, and early memories make what is occurring between client and therapist seem very familiar.

There are moments in therapy when the therapist fails to be empathic. Kohut first noticed the consequences with Miss F., who not only refused his insightful interpretations but then angrily proclaimed: "You are ruining my analysis with these interpretations" (Kohut, 1971). At first Kohut, like a classical analyst, interpreted this as resistance. Then he realized he was failing to be empathic, imposing his interpretations on her situation. He learned two things from repeated incidents like this. First, he had to stop making the interpretations and permit the analysand to articulate her needs. Second, the therapist's failures to empathize duplicates the early parental failures and sets off depressive or angry reactions in the analysand. Thus the analytic or therapeutic situation can reactivate the thwarted developmental process. If the therapist manages the moment of failed empathy correctly, he or she can facilitate inner structure building and a better-integrated self can develop, one that does not need to use people as self-objects but that can form much better relationships with others and can rely more on inner resources in times of need.

5. *The criteria for termination and the management of the termination phase are altered accordingly.* As therapists probe

more deeply and link current complaints to earlier phases of childhood, they of course find more grist for the therapeutic mill. Then they insist that the new issues be worked through before therapy can be properly terminated. Thus Reich hopes to see lasting signs of real character change before terminating, and Melanie Klein insists that the conflicts and anxieties of the first year of life be worked through before agreeing it is time to terminate.

As I mentioned in chapter 2, the lengthening of the therapy and greater dependency on the therapist mean that at termination, separation and loss issues loom larger and require more attention. The opposite trend toward briefer therapies has another set of implications for termination: the date for the last session is usually set at the commencement of the therapy, and the client's reactions to the brevity of treatment become part of the material to be worked through (see chapter 5). In either case, the changes in symptom lists, diagnostic categories, and treatment techniques bear heavily on the conduct of the termination.

Kohut (1977) compares his criteria for termination with Freud's. For Freud, with neurotic patients, the question is whether or not the oedipal conflicts—that is, the conflicts among the ego, the id and the superego, all basically viable intrapsychic structures—have been resolved. According to Kohut (1977):

> When we turn to the narcissistic personality disorders, however, we are no longer dealing with the pathological results of unsatisfactory solutions of conflicts between structures that are in essence intact, but with forms of psychological malfunctioning arising in consequence of the fact that the central structures of the personality—the structures of the self—are defective. And so, in the narcissistic personality disorders, our description of the process and goals of psychoanalysis and of the conditions that characterize a genuine termination (under what circumstances we can say that the analytic task has been completed) must therefore be based on a definition of the nature and location of the essential psychological defects and on a definition of their cure. (pp. 2–3)

Kohut presents a series of cases and discusses termination in each. He stresses the way developments in the transference provide opportunities for gradual transmuting internalization and inner structure formation until the point is reached where a better-consolidated self permits the analysand to relate to the analyst as an autonomous object, not a mirroring or idealized self-object. By this time, the analysand is capable of experiencing joy and exuberance, has a capacity for internal regulation of self-esteem, is capable of empathy and therefore can be truly intimate, and has creative outlets.

Kohut (1977) generalizes the last item into the critical criterion for termination:

> The psychoanalytic treatment of a case of narcissistic personality disorder has progressed to the point of its intrinsically determined termination (has brought about the cure of the disorder) when it has been able to establish one sector within the realm of the self through which an uninterrupted flow of the narcissistic strivings can proceed toward creative expression—however limited the social impact of the achievements of the personality might be and however insignificant the individual's creative activity might appear to others. (pp. 53–54)

6. *It is argued that the technique and the approach to termination are the specific indicated treatment for this particular diagnostic category.* Each innovator believes she or he has discovered the correct way to understand the phenomenon under study and to treat the emotional condition. This kind of confidence is required if one is to publish the work and gain prominence as a teacher of the technique.

The debates between Otto Kernberg and Heinz Kohut are quite instructive in this regard. In his attempts to prove that his approach to narcissism is more correct, Kernberg (1975, 1984) spells out the differences between the two theories and tells how he and Kohut would practice therapy differently. In their responses to Kernberg's criticisms, self psychologists (Ornstein, 1974; Wolf, 1983) are forced to clarify some of the imprecise points in their arguments. And by reading both sides of the debate (Adler, 1986), clinicians gain further understanding.

The same certainty characterizes the cognitive therapists, who argue that theirs is the best treatment for depression; the brief therapists, who argue theirs is the treatment of choice for adjustment disorders or posttraumatic stress disorders; and so forth. With each claiming to have the answer for treating one or more mental conditions, is it any wonder there is support in the mental-health professions for a treatment manual that outlines the indicated treatments for the particular diagnositc categories?

In its general outline, the clinical logic goes something like this: The more severe the psychopathology, the earlier the developmental trauma and fixation, the more primitive the defense mechanisms typically employed, the deeper the therapy must go to be effective, the longer the therapy is likely to run, and the more problematic the separation issues at termination. At one end of the spectrum is long-term therapy for the psychoses and severe character disorders; at the other, brief therapy for certain neurotic conditions and life crises. This is the logic.

Kohut's "The Two Analyses of Mr. Z." (1979) illustrates this logic perfectly. Kohut demonstrates that a psychoanalysis that is informed by self psychology is far superior to a classical analysis when it comes to treating the narcissistic personality. Mr. Z. was in analyses of both kinds—both conducted by Heinz Kohut, as a matter of fact. Mr. Z. first entered analysis with Kohut in his mid-twenties, when Kohut "was viewing analytic material entirely from the point of view of classical analysis" (p. 3). That first analysis lasted about four years. There followed an interval of five and a half years, after which Mr. Z. returned to undergo another analysis that lasted four more years. Kohut conducted that second analysis with a "new frame of reference": self psychology. From his new stance, Kohut could look back and decide that although there was significant symptomatic improvement in the first analysis, it was really nothing but a "transference success," no real structural change occurred, and therefore it is not surprising that Mr. Z. would encounter enough difficulties to return for a second analysis.

In the second analysis, presumably because Kohut did not make oedipal and resistance interpretations but rather let the mirroring and idealizing transferences play themselves out, the analysis penetrated to further depths. Mr. Z. became aware of ways his engulfing mother used him as her object and never really responded to his needs, and ways his own masochism was an attempt to compensate for a weak and fragmented self. By the termination of this second analysis, he was able to forgive his mother and was better able to empathize with her plight. In other words, the first analysis did not reach deep enough and did not alter the inner structure of the self sufficiently to provide a lasting cure, but the second did.

In another context, Kohut (1977) claims that not only is a long-term analysis of the self indicated in the kinds of cases that he is treating, but it is actually predetermined that the analysis go on for as long as it does: "A genuine termination, it may be added here, is not brought about by external manipulation. Like the transference, it is predetermined; correct psychoanalytic technique can do no more than allow it to evolve" (pp. 48–49).

Is it any wonder it starts to seem, to clinician and client alike, as if the client's condition, and the rate of progress of the therapy, determine a "correct" moment for termination—that is, as if all the two need to know is the condition being treated, and how well the therapy is progressing, to determine when it is appropriate to call a halt to the treatment. When the client asks the therapist whether it is time to end, the hope implicit in the question is that the therapist, basing his or her opinion on an understanding of all the latest theories and techniques, can give a definite answer.

As will become apparent in the chapters that follow, there are contradictions in the clinical logic. One is the discrepency between clinical and fiscal considerations. According to the clinical logic, one's mental condition should determine the length of one's therapy. In fact, the much more important consideration is one's financial resources. Instead of offering longer-term therapy to the clients with the most severe disorders, the clinician is likely to advise the client with sufficient means to undergo long-term therapy and the one with less financial resources to make the best of brief therapy, even if the latter client suffers from a more severe disturbance than the former. In order to explore this contradiction—one rarely touched on in the clinical literature—I will turn from the discussion of long-term, open-ended therapy to the brief, time-limited variety. A discussion of brief therapy will also provide new perspective on the termination issue.

Chapter 5

The Brief-Therapy Alternative

WHEN FREUD (1937) told the Wolfman his analysis would end one year hence, he opened the door to brief therapy, even though it was in this same essay that he debunked Otto Rank's attempt to shorten psychoanalysis. It seems that the first three years of the Wolfman's analysis were nowhere near as productive as that final year, when they worked under a strict time limit. Brief therapists, most of the prominent ones themselves trained as psychoanalysts, are essentially proposing that, in the treatment of certain conditions, the first several years of open-ended analysis are dispensable, and the whole therapy can be reduced to that time-limited and accelerated terminal phase.

There are three reasons for including a chapter on brief therapy in this discussion of termination. First, the time limits imposed by brief therapists tend to exaggerate certain termination issues. Second, it is an opportunity to make the discussion of termination more inclusive. That is, until now the discussion has been about psychoanalysis or long-term psychotherapy, and about the tendency for therapies to lengthen as time goes on and more conditions are considered amenable to therapeutic intervention. Brief therapy represents a countertendency, almost a backlash against the lengthening of therapies. Therefore, by including a chapter on brief therapy, I extend the scope of my discussion beyond the long-term variety of therapy. The third reason for including a chapter on brief therapy is that it serves to expose the contradiction between the clinical logic of termination and the fact that means more than clinical condition seem to determine the length of one's therapy.

The advent of brief therapy is consistent with the clinical logic of termination. The list of symptoms is circumscribed, preferably with an identifiable time of onset in the not-too-distant past. The diagnosis is of an acute and not-too-severe neurotic conflict or crisis, the method being inappropriate for psychotic conditions, severe character disturbances, and suicidal or substance-abusing clients. The theory borrows heavily from Freud's early work, especially his emphasis on oedipal conflicts. The technique is very specific, involving a sharp focus on certain issues, particularly as they surface in the transference. The termination of therapy is designed to work in the context of a time-limited and focal therapy. And the advocates of brief therapy certainly talk as if it is the treatment of choice in particular cases. All six steps of the clinical logic are represented.

I will concentrate here on one particular kind of brief therapy, the kind that has emerged directly out of the psychoanalytic experience. I am referring to the brief therapy that Malan (1976), Sifneos (1972), Davanloo (1978), and Mann (1973) have popularized in the last decade. Gustafson (1986) provides a useful summary and some contributions of his own on technique. Theoretically, it is derived from psychoanalysis: the practitioner interprets the transference as an analyst would, or focuses on oedipal conflicts as Freud would. I could enlarge the subject matter by including other kinds of brief therapy, for instance, those informed by systems theory or those that make use of "paradoxical commands." But since I have been tracing a line of development of therapy from psychoanalysis, I will restrict the discussion to the one kind of brief therapy.

Brief Psychotherapy

Judd Marmor (1979) recounts the history of brief therapy. Freud had some brief cases. For instance, he saw conductor Bruno Walter for six sessions with a successful outcome in 1906, and he cured composer Gustav Mahler's impotence in a single four-hour session in 1908. Ferenczi and Rank (1925) experimented with the technique of setting a time limit for therapy and not rescinding it. Leaving out much of the traditional analytic investigation of the past, they focused instead on the current problems and the transference relationship. Alexander and French

(1946) made some major revisions of psychoanalytic theory in the interest of briefer therapy. They questioned the long-held assumption that long therapies are necessary to attain deep and lasting cures. They reduced the frequency of sessions, made the couch optional, became more active in the treatment process, advocated enough flexibility to fit the treatment strategy to the individual case, and experimented with interruptions in the treatment designed to diminish the client's dependency on the therapist. The current generation of brief therapists follow in the tradition of these pioneers.

The idea of brief therapy is to condense certain of Freud's lessons on technique into a concentrated method that can be articulated simply and taught easily, and that promises impressive reduction of symptoms after a very short course of therapy. Not everyone wishes to be in long-term therapy, not everyone wishes to sort through all the feelings about the therapist as a transference figure and about leaving him or her, and even those who wish to cannot always afford the long hours of therapy needed to do so. The whole analytic process does not need to be repeated in every case. The therapist can concentrate the lessons of many analyses and longer-term therapies and offer the time-conscious consumer a more condensed package.

The brief therapists select clients whose emotional symptoms are circumscribed. They find an unresolved developmental issue—preferably oedipal—that can be clearly linked to the current problem, make sure they select only clients who are able to make use of the therapist's interpretation of the link and are highly motivated to change, and then aim interventions at the circumscribed symptoms and their developmental roots, making particular use of transference interpretations to do so. According to Habib Davanloo (1978), "The major task of the therapist is to understand as quickly as possible the essential problems and make them understandable to the patient . . . we cannot wait for the material to bubble up" (p. 343).

Most of the brief therapists stress selection criteria, seeking the variables that correlate most strongly with successful outcome. Thus they exclude clients who have a history of psychotic decompensation, serious suicide attempts, significant drug and alcohol abuse, and impulsive acting out. Most insist that the potential client be able to make use of an interpretation offered during the initial interview. Peter Sifneos (1972) recommends the selection of clients who have had at least one meaningful and long-lasting intimate relationship. In other words, the best outcomes occur when the client is relatively healthy, insightful, motivated to change, and unlikely to fall apart or become overly dependent. They can be skimmed off the waiting lists in public clinics, or identified in private consulting rooms, and the brief-therapy encounter will most likely be productive, while the waiting list shrinks or the private therapist quickly creates another opening in his or her busy schedule to see another client in need.

Some brief therapists literally view the entire therapy as a concentrated termination phase. This is James Mann's (1973) approach. Basing his version of brief therapy on psychoanalytic and phenomenological concepts of time, he sets a twelve-session limit, selecting a date for the final session at the beginning of treatment. He selects a focus for the therapy much as Malan, Sifneos, and Davanloo do, but then he links the focus—the circumscribed current problems as well as the related prototypic moment from childhood—to the universal issues of separation, loss, and the eventuality of death. He feels each client, is some idiosyncratic way, is conflicted about separation and death, and experiences these conflicts in relation to time. By conducting therapy in the shadow of a strict time limit, the therapist helps activate the conflicts in the therapeutic setting and has an opportunity to show the client how such concerns are related to the presenting symptoms.

From the first session, Mann keeps focusing the client's attention on the number of sessions remaining—eleven after the first, ten after the second, six after the sixth, and so forth. The client's initial excitement about how much relief therapy will bring begins to wane sometime in the middle of the therapy, when she or he realizes that the symptoms are not entirely resolved and little time remains. Then the therapist points out the counterproductive ways the client has dealt with limitations and endings or losses in the past. And finally the therapist helps the client work through the impending loss of this therapeutic relationship. Thus, termination issues are identified from the first session and linked with the presenting complaints, and the whole treatment focuses on working through issues that the time limit intensifies.

Notice that Mann's approach to time is quite the opposite of Ferenczi's concept of "timelessness" (see chapter 2). According to Ferenczi (1927), "The completion of an analysis is possible only if, so to speak, unlimited time is at one's disposal. I agree with those who think that the more unlimited it is, the greater are the chances of quick success" (p. 82).

Compare Mann's (1973) stance:

> Any psychotherapy which is limited in time brings fresh flame to the enduring presence in all persons of the conflict between timelessness, infinite time, immortality and the omnipotent fantasies of childhood on the one hand, and time, finite time, reality, and death on the other hand. The wishes of the unconscious are timeless and promptly run counter to an offer of help in which time is limited. Thus, any time-limited psychotherapy addresses itself to child time and to adult time. At the least, this gives rise to powerful conflicting reactions, responses, and most of all, conflicting expectations. The greater the ambiguity as to the duration of treatment, the greater the influence of child time on unconscious wishes and expectations. The greater the specificity of duration of treatment, the more rapidly and appropriately is child time confronted with reality and the work to be done. (p. 11)

There is a reversal here. Analyst Ferenczi creates a state of timelessness in the consulting room in order to foster exploration of the timeless unconscious. Brief therapist Mann, by fixing a time limit and then confronting what he considers excessive dependency on the the therapist, rules out that state of timelessness. The contrast raises a question: Is brief therapy a shorter version or lesser quantity of the same basic entity we know as open-ended psychoanalytic therapy, or does the change in quantity mean a change in quality? In other words, isn't the very nature of therapy altered in the abbreviating, including its aims?

Therapy contains two quite different moments: open-ended exploration of the unconscious where timelessness is very relevant, and another moment where a technique-oriented and time-bound onslaught against resistances is called for (Kupers, 1986).

I illustrated these two moments in chapter 1, in Freud's case reports. Freud functioned more as a technician when he confronted Dora, detectivelike, about her knowledge of oral sex. Later, he was more the explorer when he confessed that he would never have guessed the Wolfman's association of a butterfly with a woman's spreading her legs. The therapist, at one moment functioning as a technician, stresses sharp observation, accurate data gathering, rigorous psychodynamic formulation, exact diagnosis, precise interpretation, and objective measurement of outcome.

At another moment, the therapist functions as an explorer, being more interested in an unrestricted search for fantasies and meanings, in discovering what is unique, and what potential there is for growth and healing residing within the individual. The technician is cheered by the closeness of fit between the client's behavior and what theory would predict. It is the explorer who "surprises" (Winnicott, 1971b) the client and himself with the results. There are moments in any therapy when the therapist must be firm, insist his or her interpretation is correct, and help the client look at the reasons for resistance. At other moments the therapist must back down or remain silent, let the client discover the meaning and be surprised by the discovery. The point is to fit the therapeutic approach to the needs of the client and the therapeutic moment rather than trying to fit the client into the single available approach. Ideally, the therapist combines the best of both approaches.

There is a tendency among brief therapists to stress technique over exploration. This is what the time limit accomplishes. After all, if the therapist seeks a thorough history in the first interview, quickly makes a dynamic formulation to inform a strategy of focal and sharp intervention, and ends the therapy soon after the presenting symptoms abate, there is little or no time to explore anything that is not directly related to the focus. This is in contrast to the open-ended time frame of longer-term therapy or analysis, which provides an opportunity to explore in depth the individual's history, the contents of his or her unconscious, and the patterns of defense. Then the analyst can offer well-considered interventions, and the shape of the new self will evolve out of the analytic process, not as prescribed by the analyst in advance. This is not to say that psychoanalysis is without problems—for example, the problem of interminability. The only point I want to make about this for now is that time-limited and open-ended therapies are quite different and that this difference is more than quantitative. Further on, I will describe how the two different therapies are distributed inequitably according to class.

I will mention one other concern I have. The advocates of brief therapy make it clear that their approach works only with a very select client population, for instance, people who seem unlikely to be harmed. Then the therapist can proceed to batter down resistances and facilitate rapid psychological change. Brief therapy utilizes this capability very effectively. Perhaps a therapist must be this aggressive if she or he expects big changes in a short time. But then the aggression itself is a variable to be considered in the evaluation of outcome. Some symptoms may be diminished, but other important issues will be ignored. For instance, the client might accept the therapist's insights without looking at feelings of discomfort in relating to such an insistent and intrusive therapist. Some of these feelings are suppressed, just as they were in earlier relationships with intrusive or intimidating parents, so the seemingly symptom-free client can leave therapy with little insight into this dimension of her or his difficulties in relationships. Often it is just this kind of insight that would permit a previously compliant individual to question his or her external circumstances. Winnicott offers an alternative approach. Many of his therapies are brief. Yet he is very much the explorer, permitting his clients to discover their own interpretations (Winnicott, 1971 a and b, Gustafson, 1983, and Kupers, 1986). In any case, brief therapy can be quite effective.

The Hospital Porter

I had the opportunity to treat a client with supervision by David Malan at the Tavistock Institute in London in the early 1970s (reported in Malan, 1976, pp. 321–25). The client, a twenty-five-year-old hospital porter, had lost at least one hundred jobs since graduating high school, usually because he fought the authority of supervisors. His marriage of several years was troubled because of his job instability, and because he drank excessively and was depressed when not drunk.

The man was very bright. In fact, one reason for his depression was that he had done so little with his intelligence. He was very aware of the link between unresolved feelings toward his father and his trouble with authority figures. During his intake interview, the interviewer suggested that behind his overt hostility there might be a wish to restore a warm relationship he had once had with his father and lost. He was very moved by this interpretation, and this is what convinced us that this man might do well in brief therapy with a focus on his ambivalence toward his father and other authority figures.

Of course, the ambivalence emerged in the transference. First, he would express appreciation when I offered a helpful interpretation, and then he would attack me because I was not doing all I could to relieve his depression and make him feel better. As we explored the similarities between this kind of ambivalence and early feelings of disappointment in his father, a pattern of his work life became evident: he would drive a boss into a corner with his intellect, provoke the intimidated boss to threaten him with dismissal, say he did not care about the job, and end up being fired. By focusing on the self-destructiveness contained in this single dynamic, demonstrating its roots in early conflicts with father, and monitoring its repetition in the transference, we were able to work through the man's need to be belligerent at work. He began to hold down a steady job, and consequently felt less depression and less need to drink.

The termination of therapy was uneventful. We had agreed in advance on a date for the final session. Partly because the client had been selected and did not demonstrate serious "oral/dependency" issues, partly because the boundaries of the therapeutic relationship were clear from the beginning and the client was planning to end therapy at a predetermined date, and partly because we worked through the clients' mild feelings that he was not getting enough from his therapist, when the date approached the client was able to express appreciation for the gains of therapy, say that he would miss me, and then warmly say goodbye. The symptomatic relief was sufficient to call the therapy a success without our ever touching on the man's other conflicts and character traits. (Later he would return for more psychotherapy because of marital tensions).

When clients are well selected and proper therapeutic technique is employed, the gains from a brief course of therapy can be quite impressive. But there is another side to the picture.

The Social Uses of Brief Therapy

Remember, the brief therapists insist that successful outcome depends on proper selection of candidates. They explicitly warn against offering brief therapy to people suffering from a severe character disorder such as borderline character. In fact, failure often results when brief therapy is offered to this group. The client feels too much resentment about the time limitations and what she or he perceives as the eventual desertion by the therapist to benefit from what can be accomplished even within those parameters. Such clients might terminate therapy angrily and regress, or undo or sabotage all the gains that have been accomplished. Similarly, the brief therapists exclude alcoholics, ex-psychotics, and so on. There is a logic to this selection protocol. It takes a very special type of person to benefit from psychodynamic therapy offered in very small parcels.

In practice, the selection criteria differ from those the innovators recommend. For instance, in many mental health clinics—in the public sector, or the clinics of private health plans—an administrative decision is made that in light of budget limitations, and in order to distribute fairly the limited amount of available services, everyone who requests talking therapy will be assigned to a twelve- or a twenty-session course of brief therapy. Then, in spite of very clear selection criteria in the literature, the therapist in the public setting is faced with the prospect of seeing all clients who walk in—some of whom are suicidal, alcoholic, or borderline—in some form of brief therapy. The guidelines for practicing therapy break down, usually in the direction of employing more confrontation of resistance and permitting less unstructured exploration—that is, technique becomes even more dominant.

This scenario of grossly violated selection criteria is well known today. It occurs in public clinics, including county, state, and federal community mental-health centers; it occurs in large pre-paid private health facilities; and increasingly, as private insurance companies limit the number of therapy sessions covered, it is occurring in the private clinician's office. Many insurance companies in the United States pay half or two-thirds of a certain maximum allowable fee schedule for a strictly limited number of sessions of therapy, and many clients tell their therapists at the beginning that they cannot continue in therapy after their coverage runs out. Thus the therapist is pressured to offer some form of brief therapy—again regardless of clinical selection criteria.

The pattern developing in regard to brief therapy is reminiscent of the pattern involving crisis intervention in the United States in the 1960s. Directors of the newly funded community mental health centers sought a therapeutic modality that could be offered to the large population their clinics were mandated to serve. The crisis-intervention model seemed to fit the spirit of the times, as well as the budget. The therapist and client have six visits to focus on the client's crisis, help the client ventilate the feelings or mourn, and then the symptoms should be sufficiently alleviated for the client to return to his or her prior level of functioning (Caplan, 1961). The therapist is instructed not to dwell on childhood histories, not to interpret transference reactions, and not to expect characterological change. The technique is quite a contrast to today's brief therapy (with the exception of Horowitz's work—see below), where transference interpretations are critical. The aim is merely a return to the prior homeostasis.

The crisis-intervention model can work very well. A woman complains she has been lethargic and unable to pursue her writing career since her mother died a year ago. The therapist tells her the problem is a morbid grief reaction, and she needs to pay attention to unresolved conflicts with her mother and unexpressed feelings. She does so for six weeks. With the therapist's support, she permits herself to think about her mother, recalls how much she hated her once, and feels the rage. At another time she remembers the loving way her mother waited for her to come home from school and gave her a snack to help her get through her homework assignment. She cries. She lets herself miss her mother. She may never work through all her complex feelings about her mother, but she works through enough to be able to continue in her life. This is a successful outcome.

In practice, a different fate awaited the model. Even during the 1960s' Kennedy-initiated "war on poverty," funding for mental-health services in low-income communities was never sufficient, and the simultaneous closing of state mental hospitals effectively flooded the newly built community mental-health centers with clients (see Chu and Trotter, 1974). Many centers routinely offered every new client six sessions of crisis intervention, and then the ones who were not cured would be assigned to group therapies. The figures seemed to work out. Every six weeks a therapist would have another slot open to accept a new client. The clinic waiting list would shrink. The only problem was that successful outcomes were more the exception than the rule. After all, not all the clients who requested services suffered from an identifiable loss or crisis, so there was no clinical logic to fitting them into a six-session therapy format. While the model could be shown to be effective when used with clients who fit its selection criteria, the outcomes in community mental-health centers were disappointing.

Like crisis intervention, brief therapy was developed to solve the problem of crowded waiting rooms and long waiting lists. But the innovators devised their methodologies for a small proportion of those waiting lists, insisting that unsuitable clients be offered other treatment modalities. Today clinicians are pressured by financial considerations to fit more clients into the brief-therapy format. Administrators in public agencies, private health provider corporations, and insurance companies are happy: now they can give a rationale for a limit to benefits and train their staffs to practice only these time-limited techniques. Meanwhile, as in the case of crisis intervention, many clients who do not fit the selection criteria, even clients for whom brief therapy is contraindicated, will be offered only ten or twenty sessions. Thus the client, on the basis of means, is fit into the therapeutic modality rather than the other way around.

It is one thing for clinicians, confronted by an externally mandated time limit, to make the best of the situation by developing a technique to treat people in a shorter time frame, all the while protesting that it is inequitable and not the best way to conduct therapy. It is quite another to make an unfortunate restriction of services seem a virtue. Too often clinicians, when told that because of fiscal considerations they will have to treat certain clients in a much shortened time frame, go along happily, believing as they do that the innovations in therapeutic technique they come up with are a boon to society.

It is in this context that clinicians begin to enlarge their claims for the efficacy of brief therapy. For instance, consider the progression of Mardi Horowitz's research from 1976 to 1984. He and his group of clinicians-researchers at the University of California, San Francisco, have devised a very creative strategy for treating the after-effects of extreme and traumatic stress in people with very different underlying character structures (1976). They tailor their interventions to the particular personality of the stressed individual, providing one kind of intervention when the underlying personality is hysterical and a different intervention when it is obsessional or narcissistic—but each time, the intervention is aimed at the stress disorder, leaving the underlying character structure intact. Like crisis intervention, the aim is a return to the previous homeostasis, not a change of character. Horowitz and his group have enjoyed well-deserved acclaim for their success with posttraumatic stress disorder.

But soon they began to expand claims for the efficacy of brief therapy. They even outline a strategy for the brief treatment of the borderline character (Horowitz et al., 1984). In other words, if the brief, intensive technique works in the case of posttraumatic stress disorders, perhaps it will work with deeper-lying and longer-held psychopathology. As if in direct rebuttal, Otto Kernberg, a pioneer of long-term therapy with the borderline character, comments (1984): "The expectation that our increasing knowledge will shorten the psychological treatment of severe character pathology and the borderline disorders may represent one more illusion about the process, technique, and outcome of psychotherapy," (pp. 252–53).

The point is that inequities in the distribution of psychotherapy services directly contradict the clinical logic of termination. According to that logic, people suffering from the most severe emotional disorders should undergo the longest and most deep-probing therapy. In actuality, it is means and not clinical condition that usually determines the length and depth of one's therapy. Those who can afford private fees are encouraged to undergo long-term therapy—and of course theories evolve to explain why high-functioning but unhappy people, perhaps with a psychotic core deep within, should be in long-term therapy. Meanwhile, those of lesser means are relegated to time-limited therapy slots, regardless of the severity of their clinical condition—and other theories evolve to explain how brief therapy can alleviate the severe disorder. The contradiction is highlighted when some of the clinicians who practice and write about brief therapy, being psychoanalysts themselves, go from their jobs at universities or public clinics to their private practices in the suburbs, where they offer longer-term therapy or analysis to clients who have lesser symptoms but greater ability to pay.

In *Public Therapy* (Kupers, 1981) I described a double standard in mental-health-care delivery, whereby talking therapy is available to those who can afford the fees while those who cannot are medicated or involuntarily hospitalized when their problems get out of hand. Brief therapy occupies a middle position in this schema. It is generally available to people who work and have health coverage, but whose coverage is limited. Blue-collar, service, and clerical workers fit this description. Their health plans usually limit the number of therapy sessions covered—but unlike the unemployed, they have access to some talking therapy. Students fit the description too, since many university health services offer time-limited therapy services. More affluent people either have deluxe health insurance plans that cover more therapy sessions, or they can afford to pay private fees for the psychoanalysis or psychotherapy they elect to undergo.

Chapter 6

Therapy in Pieces

DOES BRIEF therapy represent a countermovement to the tendency I discussed (chapters 2 and 3) for therapies to lengthen? Is it just that the health-plan administrators and insurance adjusters have found a way to justify reduced payments for psychotherapy? Certainly the advent of brief therapy does these things very nicely. But it does something more. The brief-therapy modality has arrived at just the right time. Where psychoanalysis might be conceived of as a once-in-a-lifetime endeavor, psychotherapy is not usually consumed at one sitting. The average therapy consumer probably undergoes relatively brief stints of psychotherapy at several different times in his or her lifetime. More and more, clients enter therapy wishing to work through one or another circumscribed issue, end the therapy when they feel satisfied with the immediate results, and then return to be in therapy again when another crisis arises. It is hard to say which came first, the brief therapy or the pattern whereby more and more people begin to utilize therapy in pieces over a lifetime. Whichever it is, the whole meaning of termination changes.

The Moment of Ambivalence

There is a moment in just about every therapy when the original symptoms that brought the client in have diminished sufficiently for the client to pause to consider whether further therapy is needed. Some clients are entirely ambivalent about therapy in the first place, for fear of stigma, because they have no knowledge of what to expect, or because the prospect of a deepening relationship with the therapist frightens them. They are likely to take the opportunity abruptly and unilaterally to discontinue the treatment. Others are willing to talk about their ambivalence, or their lack of clarity about what more therapy might accomplish and why they should continue to attend. Sometimes, when the client is ambivalent about leaving therapy, and until that ambivalence is resolved, the therapist must simply dig in his heels and interpret the client's resistance to a deepening therapeutic relationship. I did so with Alan.

Alan

Alan, a forty-one-year-old professional man, came to see me seeking help. "I believe I love my wife. I'm having an affair with my secretary. I think I love her—maybe even more than I love my wife. My wife is starting to catch on. She's getting really upset and making all kinds of demands. I'm a wreck, and I don't know what to do!" I asked this father of three children how he felt about all this, and he replied, "I don't know how I feel. That's the problem. And I don't know what I want to do. That's why I've come to see you."

He had been a great success at everything. A star athlete and "straight A" student in high school, he joined a fraternity in college and married his college sweetheart before going off to graduate school. She became pregnant immediately—later he admits that she was pregnant when they were married, and he often thinks about what his life would have been like if they had not married so young. The young couple adopted a pattern that lasted from then on: he studied or worked, she raised the children and attended to the house. He went to prestigious schools, developed good "connections," and became successful and wealthy.

As he talked about his "connections," it became clear his associations with people were mainly pragmatic. He was unable to identify for me any real friend he could rely on. He assumed that since he basically was using people to get ahead, they were all using him too. In fact, the only person he really trusted and talked to about anything of significance was his secretary, June.

"I never had an affair until now. I don't want to let go of June—she's fast becoming my best friend and confidant. Susan [his wife] is really being unreasonable. She stamps and screams at me, she can't sleep all night, she refuses sex, and by now she's guessed it's June I'm seeing and insists I never see her again. I try to assure her that I'm not going to have sex with her again." As he completed this part of his story, he sank back in his chair, sighed, and said, "This whole business has been blown out of proportion. I feel like I've lost all control of my life. I just wish it would all go away."

On the first visit, Alan did not look depressed. He was very energetic in his attempts to tell me his story and convince me that though he was confused, the real trouble was the women and their unreasonable feelings. By the third visit, after he had committed himself to undergo some ongoing psychotherapy, he began to demonstrate some sadness and admit to being depressed. "I feel empty. I don't want to leave my wife because that would mean leaving the children. I'm scared to be alone. June is fifteen years younger than me. I think I love her, but I feel silly robbing the cradle like that, and besides, there's too much of a gap in experience and sophistication between us. It would never work. I'm really bummed out."

Our first three or four sessions of therapy were filled with Alan's anxiety. He became almost exhilarated in telling me about his romantic situation. But he quickly concluded that leaving his wife for his newfound love would not work. Because of the difference in age, he was afraid that their affair would end and he would find himself all alone. The following session focused on his fantasy of dropping everything—career, family, possessions—and going off somewhere far away. He decided that would not work either. He began to seriously reconsider the wisdom of leaving his wife. He cried for the first time in many years.

In the following session, all the progress we had made locating Alan's feelings seemed to be lost. He was stiff, distant, and unable to tell me what was going on. I asked, "Could it be that you have regrets about sharing your tears with me, that you are afraid that now other uncomfortable feelings will emerge if we go on in therapy?" He flatly denied there was any validity in such questions. He continued to attend, but he seemed more numb, more the dispassionate storyteller.

After two months in therapy, Alan decided to stay with his wife. His anxiety diminished. He began to settle back into his prior state of numbness. Meanwhile, after responding very well to interpretations in the first several sessions and seeming motivated to look at his life and make changes, he began to disregard my interventions, and on several occasions seemed intent on devaluing me. For instance, he commented about the mediocrity of my taste in clothes and speculated that many of my other clients were probably "dependent types."

Though Alan did not say anything direct about it, it was clear that by this point in his therapy the crisis was past and he was thinking about terminating. Meanwhile, I was thinking about how I would respond when the question came up. Alan was in something of a midlife crisis when he first came to see me. It was not just the affair. Not every affair is a midlife crisis, and many people experience midlife crises without acting them out sexually. It was his barely awakening realization that he did not know what he felt, did not know his own desires, and that this state of affairs was no longer tolerable. He experienced a deep dissatisfaction with his life and his relationships—a dissatisfaction that, after two months of therapy, he realized was deeper than sexual frustration.

But Alan also presented with an underlying character disorder, a narcissistic personality. It was not only his conflicts about relationships, his tendency to use people, and his dread of being used by others. He would also tend to idealize me at times— like when my interpretations hit home—and then there were those times when he swung around and completely devalued me. Linked with such fluctuations in his appraisal of my worth was a running evaluation of his own. When he was complimenting me on the perceptiveness of my interpretations, he said he felt safe being in therapy with me and felt more competent and powerful at work. When he was criticizing my wardrobe, he was also thinking he was really only as successful as he was because he was fooling people, manipulating them into thinking he was competent at what he did. And he seemed incapable of real mourning. When a friend betrayed him, ending the friendship, he would write it off: "The guy wasn't really important to me anyway." But Alan was only interested in resolving his ambivalence about relationships with two women when he entered therapy.

Should I focus on Alan's immediate crisis, and as soon as he resolves his ambivalence terminate the therapy, considering it a successful brief therapy aimed at resolving a midlife crisis? Or should I insist that the crisis represents only the tip of the iceberg, interpret his wish to terminate as a resistance to the deepening of our therapeutic relationship, and use my influence to persuade him to continue in long-term therapy with the aim of characterological change? Here is a situation where a therapist might be colluding with a client's resistance to therapy by agreeing to a brief time limit. By the time the twelve- or twenty-session limit is reached, someone as closed off to feelings and frightened of intimacy as Alan might be just beginning to open up. If I agree to cut the therapy short, I might well be colluding with his defensive need to end this therapeutic relationship before it gets threateningly close, and an opportunity would be lost to examine why this man short-circuits every deepening relationship. Of course, if Alan's financial situation only permitted twelve or twenty sessions, my clinical opinion about all this would be irrelevant.

Before I had this question resolved in my own mind, it became apparent that Alan's motivation to continue in therapy was waning. Still he said nothing direct about the issue, so finally I commented: "Now that you've given up the idea of leaving Susan, you probably want all your dissatisfactions with married life to disappear, and you're probably even thinking about dropping out of therapy."

"Yeah, you're right! How'd you know that?" My ability to come up with a correct interpretation seemed, for the moment, to put an end to the devaluing.

"Well, I'm the one you've told all your inner thoughts to. You said you told no one else, certainly not your wife, how much you loved June. You told me all about your dissatisfactions, how unbearable the boredom in your life is. Now that you're considering patching things up at home, it makes sense that you want to be rid of me." At this point, Alan said he had been seriously considering ending the therapy but would not be closed to hearing what recommendations I had.

During our conversation, I decided that my influence was significant and that for Alan to drop out of therapy would be a mistake. So I shared that opinion with him. I told him that the acute crisis might be resolving, and that was to his credit, but that his dissatisfactions ran deeper. And he might as well spend some more time in therapy now with a good prospect of resolving some deeper-lying issues—for example, his ambivalence about trusting friendships—and maybe prevent some repetitions of this kind of crisis. Alan thought about it for a week and returned having decided to take my advice and enter into a long-term therapy with the aim of resolving some of his underlying conflicts.

Sometimes, when that moment arrives, the crisis is past, and the client is more set on ending the therapy. Sometimes it is best for the therapist to make a quick and graceful exit from the client's life, hoping that the client will return at a later time if the need arises. This is what I did with Ann.

Ann

Ann was forty when she came to my office complaining of depression. As we talked, she shared with me the dissatisfactions she felt within her marriage (her husband was never affectionate with her and was likely having a long-term affair) and in her career (she had dropped out of a successful professional practice in order to have time to raise three boys, currently teenagers, and was worried that she would never be able to be successful again in the world of work). She had come across a book in a bookstore, *Men Who Hate Women and the Women Who Love Them* (Forward and Torres, 1986), and found she fit the picture of a masochistic woman who is all too willing to tolerate victimization by a misogynist. She wished to get over her depression, she said, but not to end her marriage.

We talked about her situation. She explained that she was frightened of being alone and that fear pushed her to remain with her husband in spite of abuse she suffered at his hands. I helped her link that situation to her early ambivalence toward her father. She loved him dearly, but he was often rejecting. But then, in those moments of closeness—like when he hugged her after she had hit a home run in a girl's baseball tournament—she felt as if all the negative interactions were worth it.

The rewards were infrequent, the criticisms and angry reactions from her father the more usual. She had real conflicts about the kind of relationship she was in now, a repeat of the earlier one, where the male partner is intermittently abusive but otherwise very nice, and for fear that she would otherwise never gain his approval and love, she is willing to stay with him to the bitter end. We talked about all this.

She began to stand up to her husband more. The first few times we met after she had stood up to him on some little point, she would typically enter the consulting room in a state of severe depression. Asked why she was so depressed, she would answer that she and her husband had just had a big fight. So, why wasn't she angry at him, why depressed? That turned out to be a good question. We talked about that. Gradually, she became stronger. We met weekly for about six months. Her depression had progressively lightened, though it would never disappear altogether. She wanted to terminate therapy at that point. Our discussion about that uncovered her wish to stop elevating the struggle with her husband. She had found a happy-enough medium. She now knew when to compromise and when some point of contention was worth an angry battle. He backed off from her for fear of her anger—and maybe because he sensed she felt stronger and might actually leave him—and this created enough distance so that, even though he was still occasionally mean and never showed any real caring, the new equilibrium was manageable. Besides, with my encouragement, she had begun to spend more time with friends away from the house and family and was even thinking about part-time work.

Ann wanted to end the therapy immediately. In fact, she first told me about this over the phone, adding that she would not be coming to our next appointment and would not be coming in anymore. I convinced her to come in at least once more to talk about this. Interestingly, this woman had used my interpretations very often and aptly during the course of the therapy. As soon as she had decided to end treatment, she discarded that way of thinking altogether. She told me she had stopped writing down and analyzing her dreams. And she had stopped selecting for friends people who "needed to psychologize everything." In other words, her use of "the therapeutic" was time-limited—she would spend just enough time pursuing the inner quest to re-solve a crisis in her life—and once she regained her equilib-rium, she would have no further use for it. I asked whether she would be willing to come to two or three more appointments so that we could sum up and talk about our parting. She agreed do to that.

Unlike Alan, who wanted to know my opinion on the matter, Ann was set on terminating therapy. Clearly she was afraid that further exploration would threaten her tenuous marriage, and even if I said nothing about her needing to leave an unsatisfac-tory relationship, somewhere inside she knew that would have to be the next step if she were ever to be really happy. She felt it was a waste of time, knowing that, to be sitting for hours talking with me about how she feels about her life and how she is repeating patterns from her childhood with an abusive father.

I found myself, in those last few sessions, trying to get the message across to Ann that it was her decision to end therapy, just as it was her choice what she wanted to do about her mar-riage, but I wanted her to know she could return to see me whenever she felt a need. Obviously she was projecting some of her self-criticisms onto me and then assuming I disapproved of her choices. Rather than standing firm as I had done with Alan and confirming her projection that I would judge her neg-atively for ending therapy, I opted to interpret her projections and try to keep the door open for further work in the future.

Serial "Pieces of Work"

In effect, I did a piece of therapeutic work with Ann. Though we did not arrive at a termination date at the outset, and I did not stick to a focus the whole time, it was a brief therapy. The texts on brief therapy stress clarity about boundaries and time limits. They recommend setting a date for termination long in advance, and they even suggest that the client should not en-gage in any other kind of therapy for a certain period—perhaps a year or two—after the termination of the brief therapy, so that there will be an opportunity for the therapy to take effect, and perhaps for the therapist to assess the outcome.

In practice, things are rarely this clear. Studies show that clients go in and out of therapy quite frequently and move from brief to long-term therapy in other than the recommended way. Remember Frank B. (chapter 2), who began therapy anew, albeit a diluted form of therapy, with another psychiatrist almost immediately after terminating his eight-year analysis. Patterson et al. (1977) found in their study of brief-therapy clients that sixty percent had previously undergone some other form of therapy and sixty percent would reenter some form of therapy within a year of terminating the brief therapy. This and other similar studies show that clients return repeatedly for one or another form of therapy as they experience the need. Patterson comments:

> Such data suggest that psychotherapy, whether long or short in duration, whether aimed at problem resolution or character change, is not constructed by the patient as a definitive and curative process, but one which has use and value at times of need. It is uncommon, however, for therapists to structure their relationships with their patients in a way that anticipates this pattern. Most commonly, such relationships are structured as closed ended. (p. 365)

In other words, the therapist is aiming for a resolution of the transference and a definitive termination for every therapy, but in many instances, the client intends to be in therapy only until the symptoms are resolved and might plan to return when these or other symptoms become a problem again.

Gerald Amada (1983) is pragmatic about this issue. He recognizes the pattern of client's entering therapy in crisis, quickly feeling better, and then not knowing what to do about ongoing therapy. He suggests that, in practice, many therapies that began as brief therapies go through an interlude after the crisis has died down, where the therapist and client fumble around looking for a focus and then proceed into a long-term, open-ended therapeutic relationship. He identifies the moment of transition: the originally sharp focus of the work becomes vague, the therapist necessarily shifts from an active interventionist during the crisis to a relatively more inactive role as facilitator of open-ended exploration, and the transference issues become relatively more important as time goes on. Amada's description fits the therapy I conducted with Alan.

Of course, many other clients, like Ann, drop out of therapy, to return, one hopes, when stresses once again overwhelm the capacity to cope. Unlike psychoanalysis, a complete psychotherapy is not usually carried out at one sitting. Of course, many clients go through several years of therapy with one therapist and then work hard on termination issues when the end draws near. This is important. When a client's lifetime pattern of therapy consumption consists of serial very brief encounters or pieces of work, a deeper therapeutic relationship is never experienced, and many of the "separation-individuation" issues (Mahler, 1972) are never examined and worked through. The therapeutic relationship never really evolves to the point where termination issues might play an important role. In general—and this must be evaluated for every individual case—a relatively long course of therapy that gets to the separation-individuation and termination issues is useful somewhere along the way, and it often turns out that by undergoing such a therapy, the client reduces his or her need for some of the shorter pieces.

Still, a life's dosage of psychotherapy is today more likely spread out over the lifetime in small pieces. For instance, one piece of work might be undertaken at the time of a divorce or business failure, another at a time when someone close dies and life becomes unbearable, and still another when the aging process seems overwhelming—for example, after a heart attack takes the wind out of one's sails. Thus, a college-educated middle-class individual reaching forty today is likely to have undergone one or two courses of personal individual therapy, has probably been in various group experiences from sensitivity groups to the more modern "trainings," perhaps has seen a couples therapist a few times while in the throes of a battle with a mate, probably has been given permission by the more important of the two individual therapists to return whenever there is need, and is likely thinking that is just what she or he will do.

Therapists create a whole new language to discuss the phenomenon. For instance, they speak of doing "a piece of work." Thus, with a client who is not motivated or cannot afford to go on in therapy past the time when the worst symptoms are some-what ameliorated, the therapist might agree to halt the therapy—not exactly a well-worked-through termination, but a reasonable time to take a break from therapy—and might leave the client with the message that a nice "piece of work" has been accomplished, and the client might want to return for further therapy when difficulties arise in the future.

There is another important factor here. Psychoanalytic therapy has been diluted in the process of its popularization. There are all forms one can select. In Freud's day, there were no sensitivity groups, not even group therapy, no couples therapy, and no family therapy. Psychoanalysis was the only show in town. So the captive audience sat it out until the bitter end. Today, there is a whole culture built around therapy. The sensitivity groups and growth experiences of the 60s introduced a generation of consumers to psychotherapy. Since, there has been body work, co-counseling, peer self-help groups (including "twelve-step programs" such as Alcoholics Anonymous and Overeaters Anonymous), intensive growth trainings like E.S.T., and so forth. I am defining therapy very broadly now. But in the course of a lifetime, the individual is likely to come into contact with many different therapies, broadly defined. The lifetime work is essentially broken into pieces, some of which are accomplished in individual, psychoanalytically informed therapy, and some in other modalities.

Other developments have kept apace of this shift in the pattern of therapy consumption. Therapists are more numerous. Clinical practice is a popular career for sensitive survivors of the 60s—it provides a place to be honest and nurturing, and the work is paid. Also, there is less stigma today. Because therapy is commonplace, almost omnipresent in our everyday lives, it is easier to obtain, and there is more knowing support from intimates while one goes through it.

For these and other reasons, there has been a shift in the pacing of psychoanalytic therapy in consumers' lives. Certainly some analysands, such as the Wolfman, returned for repeated analyses, but as a conceptual ideal, psychoanalysis was a once-in-a-lifetime venture. Now, in its various diluted forms, therapy is consumed periodically, and therefore in pieces. Thus, when we talk about length of treatment, we are comparing a total of several years on the couch in the case of psychoanalysis to perhaps the same number of accrued hours in therapy in the course of a lifetime—the latter instance is of someone who has been in several shorter personal therapies, as well as logging a number of other hours in therapists' offices in groups, with a mate, or perhaps with a child when the latter seemed out of control. It seems that, if one wants to see evidence of the average tendency for psychotherapies to lengthen today, one must look at the total accrued hours of therapy in a lifetime rather than the length of any particular piece of work.

Not infrequently, the therapist is confronted by a client who unilaterally feels his condition is sufficiently improved for him to terminate the therapy. Instead of analyzing the way the plan to terminate contains important resistances to therapy, the therapist, being pragmatic and knowing about this modern trend, is more likely than analysts once were to agree with the plan, merely adding: "The therapy is not really complete. But if you feel you want to proceed without a therapist's help for awhile, that is fine, as long as you remember you can always return if you feel you're ready to do another piece of work." I have found that it is more when the client does not seem to get that message that the therapist will confront that client about resisting treatment. If the client gets the message, the therapist as realist figures that the client will quite likely return when it is time to do the next piece of work.

In this context, brief therapy is not so much a shortened variety of therapy as it is an opportunity for people who are not familiar with "the therapeutic" to have a well-bounded trial package. Then too, it is a modality that serves well for doing the periodic "piece of work." Interestingly, when the brief therapists first arrived on the scene, more traditional psychoanalysts dismissed their outcome studies by saying that what they had achieved was a "transference cure" or a "flight into health," and that some time after termination of the brief therapy the still unresolved deeper-lying conflicts would surface anew, displaced into a new set of symptoms. The brief therapists aimed, in their early outcome studies, to rebut this traditional analytic critique. Empirical studies did eventually show that the analysts' concern was not well founded.

Peter Sifneos captures that debate in his description of a 1956 case discussion (Davanloo, 1978). The patient complained of phobias and was concerned that his upcoming wedding would be ruined by his symptoms. The brief therapy was successful, and the man married without incident. Sifneos recalls:

> This case was presented to our staff, and we were told that we had a "flight into health." Someone disagreed and said, "No, that was a transference cure." Someone else said that this was a symptom substitution and that there was a chance this fellow was going to relapse. We have a follow-up of three and a half years for him. He still had some occasional twinges of anxiety when he entered closed spaces, but he said, "I know what these things mean, and they don't bother me as much. I have learned to live with them, I am happily married and I have two children. (p. 82)

Meanwhile, the advent of brief therapy brings the triumph of the therapeutic into new classes and contexts. Then, if clients do not want to end therapy after a brief course, but want to explore their psychological make-up more deeply, and if they can afford private fees, they can go on to longer-term therapy. Brief therapy serves to recruit from among the ranks of people who never before believed in the efficacy of the talking cure, and motivates them, sometime later in their lives when financial constraints are less, to pursue a longer course of therapy, or even to join those who regularly resort to therapy whenever problems in their personal lives seem out of control. The therapeutic that triumphs takes many forms. Lengthier and deeper-probing therapies are not the only method for the therapeutic to enter the interstices of the individual psyche and the social fabric. Brief therapies that reach into the lives of a broader spectrum of people, especially when the multiple brief pieces of therapy eventually add up to more hours in a lifetime than one course of the lengthier kind, carry the message just as well.

Now we can return to the critical question about termination: On what basis is the choice made of long-term vs. brief therapy?

Clinicians, following the clinical logic of termination, would like to be able to say that clinical considerations—an individual's condition, motivation to change, progress in therapy, and so on—determine who needs and might benefit from one or another modality. In chapter 5 I showed that the ability to pay is probably a much more important consideration. But whether or not one can afford long-term talking therapy, there is another issue involved in the choice between the two modalities: what I term "abstract commitment to psychotherapy."

An Abstract Commitment to Therapy

What do I mean by abstract commitment? The commitment to be in therapy only in order to relieve a particular symptom, be it insomnia, depression, or a conflict about authority, is rather concrete. In contrast, it is an abstract commitment that motivates one to continue in the therapeutic process even after the symptoms are relieved, the rationale being that therapy will facilitate personal understanding and growth, even if the eventual outcome is not knowable at the beginning. Abstract commitment helps one remain in therapy longer and persevere through those inevitable moments when the therapy seems stuck, the therapist is off on a tangent, or the client is just plain disgusted with the lack of progress.

Assuming an equivalent ability to pay fees for private therapy, and assuming (as I have been throughout this discussion) that the client's mental condition is not so severe that some form of psychotherapy is mandatory, then the particular client's abstract commitment to therapy plays a key role in determining the length of the therapy and the terms of termination. For instance, one group of clients, such as busy executives or professionals who are in a hurry to get past troublesome symptoms and return to full functioning at work, may be interested only in a quick cure and may wish to terminate therapy as quickly as possible without exploring early childhood events, transference issues, or conflicts about dependency and termination. Another group of clients, generally college-educated with an interest in psychology and personal growth, demonstrate a sizable abstract commitment and undertake therapy as a growth experience as much as for the treatment of particular symptoms. Greenspan and Kulish (1985), in their study of premature (in the opinion of the therapist) termination of long-term psychotherapy, interviewed the ex-clients and found that they were relatively uninterested in the psychological roots of their problems, but rather felt most were due to external circumstances. And this abstract commitment is not inborn, nor accidental. It is learned. Some people cultivate an interest in psychology by taking courses, reading, or being influenced by others who are psychologically minded. Most people develop the commitment as a result of a positive experience in psychotherapy.

A New Criterion for Termination

By being pragmatic about the client's lack of motivation to stay in therapy any longer, the therapist is inadvertently shifting the criteria for termination. Now, along with the usual criteria for termination—the amelioration of most of the symptoms, the resolution of the transference, the likelihood of continued psychological growth, and the therapist's confidence that longer therapy would not add anything to the client's potential in life—the therapist also insists that the client become attuned to the psychological sphere. Before giving their blessing to termination, some therapists require evidence that the client has internalized the therapeutic message sufficiently well to be likely to return for another course of therapy when the need arises.

Therapists even say this to clients: "After we part, I won't be entirely gone from your life—you will carry me around inside your head." In effect, the reason therapists are so often willing to give their blessing to a termination that is initiated by the client long before the therapist might feel the work is entirely completed is that, if the client has the capacity to internalize this message, in all likelihood the immediate ending will not be a termination at all, in Freud's sense, but merely a break in a process that is not completed—and that might go on over a lifetime.

The idea that the client internalizes the therapist is not new, of course. Freud would put the ego in control of the super-ego and the id, and consider the person mentally healthy. Gradually, the healthy ego was assigned the additional task of continuing the analytic work. A healthy ego would be one that could apply the uncovering of the unconscious to the problems of everyday life. The concept emerges in the contemporary literature as the "self-analytic function." For instance, Herbert Gaskill (1980) writes in the *International Journal of Psychoanalysis:*

> To the degree that the unconscious sources of behaviour are understood and organized under the dominance of the reality principle, the analysand, due to internalization of *the self-analytic function*, is in a position to make more conscious and more informed decisions about his actions. This leads to the establishment of increased internal autonomy, the fundamental goal of analysis. (p. 15)

What Gaskill describes for analysts also becomes a prerequisite in order for the therapist to say that the therapy is complete. In other words, the new criterion for termination is that the client have sufficiently internalized the therapist or the therapeutic function that she or he will likely continue on her or his own the work begun in therapy, and will return for another course of therapy as the need arises.

There is even a newly invented diagnosis, unofficial to date, to fit those who are not able to demonstrate enough of the self-analytic function to make use of psychotherapy. Alexithymia is the disorder of people who are unable to speak symbolically about their inner life, are unable to express their feelings, and have an impoverished fantasy life (Sifneos, 1973). The condition is linked to psychosomatic disorders—that is, those who cannot express themselves verbally might do so through physical symptoms, and there is speculation about an organic base for alexithymia (TenHouten et al., 1986).

Thus, without any explicit statement to this effect in the professional literature, the definition of mental health has shifted to include a certain amount of abstract commitment to therapy. Then, it is assumed by clinicians, again without explicit mention in quite these terms, that the criteria for termination have not been satisfied until there is evidence of this kind of abstract commitment. This development serves the therapy industry well. The healthy individual will spread the word, for instance, by introducing intimates as well as colleagues to the benefits of therapeutic work. The definition of mental health, and the perfect way to insure a continuing clientele for therapy, come together in one formulation about the proper time to terminate a piece of therapeutic work, and the possibility of doing further pieces of work at a later date.

Chapter 7

The Community
of Therapy Consumers

As MORE people become psychologically sophisticated and prone to turn to therapists for help with each of life's dilemmas, they tend to undergo more therapy—either lengthier at one sitting, or more accrued hours over a lifetime, or both. This creates a larger pool of potential clients for therapy, causing therapists to dig deeper to find more material to analyze and to create theoretical rationales for longer-term or repeated therapies. Thus the growth of a community of willing therapy consumers significantly influences the way termination is theorized and conducted. Therefore the discussion of termination must take into account the culture of therapy consumption.

Today's clients of therapy tend to take the lessons of the consulting room out into the world. Consider the effect of therapeutic wisdom on our ideals about the way conflict should be handled in marriage. Once, fifty or one hundred years ago, disputes between partners were likely settled by appeals to authority—the husband's, of course—or by some compromise. Today, in part because of the post-60s ideal of sexual equality, in part because there are less clearly defined role expectations in primary relationships, and in no small part because so many people have undergone psychotherapy, the struggle within the relationship begins to look like what occurs in the consulting room.

Ideally at least, each partner is expected to look deeply into his or her own part in creating the conflict and consider how personal feelings and conflicts might obstruct the process of working through differences. The two try to be "open" as they talk about the tensions between them. A man might confess that the reason he rides his wife so hard is that he is threatened by her independence and competence. She may be able to cry and say she is unable to function effectively when she feels intimidated by his criticisms. Even if he does not mention that her competence reminds him of a domineering mother, and she does not share that his intimidations remind her of an abusive father, they each reflect about such things privately, separate the mate from the parent, and the whole process is modeled on what they both learned in therapy.

Thus the form of modern intimacy begins to take on attributes of the relationship between therapist and client, with, one hopes, the role of therapist shifting back and forth in the evolution of mutual dependence. And if the partners are not able to work things out, they can always "go see someone" who will point out ways each of their transferencelike distortions impede resolution of their marital tensions. Note again that, implicitly at least, this degree of dependence on therapists is considered fairly "normal" among the community of therapy consumers. In fact, as I mentioned in chapter 6, it is even incorporated into the list of criteria for termination.

There is a core group of therapists and consumers of psychotherapy within the community, and this is the group that pursues the psychological or inner quest with the greatest dedication. Typically, they would explain that they find therapy very useful with their own personal dilemmas and also derive great satisfaction from the quest itself. They are willing to resort to therapy anew whenever their unhappiness reaches a certain level or their lives seem out of control. They apply therapeutic principles in their understanding of interpersonal relations, organizational dynamics, political events, literary themes, athletic events, and artistic productions. They tend to spend a great deal of time talking about personal and psychological themes, and they are always interested in the latest psychological theory about one or another aspect of the psyche and everyday life.

The consumers of therapy exhibit varying degrees of involvement. On the periphery are the partially committed, those who undergo a number of courses of therapy in a lifetime, during life crises for example, and read pop-psychology books or analyze their own dreams when something is troubling them, but generally abandon psychology when they feel better. Others have little interest in inner exploration for its own sake but repeatedly return to therapy when they feel a need. Consider the business executive who is troubled by massive anxiety attacks—"panic disorder," according to current nomenclature—but is not interested in any of that "sentimental stuff," only agrees to visit a clinician for a few sessions to get rid of specific symptoms, and is relieved if that clinician suggests medication without therapy.

Of course there are others who would rather have nothing to do with therapy at all. Some people shun psychotherapy, as if visiting a "shrink" had to mean one was totally psychotic. Others cannot afford talking therapy, even the brief kind. And even among the strata who can afford practically unlimited amounts, not everyone wants to undergo therapy. Not everyone internalizes the message. Also, I should mention that group of clients I have not been addressing very much here, those people who undergo a great deal of therapy, not because of any abstract commitment, but because of dire need—that is, people who are so seriously disturbed, or who have such an impoverished support network, that they need almost perpetual therapy.

In any case, the people who have a certain critical mass of therapeutic sensibility seek each other out. The process is rarely articulated in these terms. Rather, members of the community select for friends others who are sufficiently "deep," "insightful," or "there." The definition of intimacy evolves to include a capacity to be open and share psychological secrets. Believers in the reigning psychological wisdom insist their intimates be psychological—perhaps they send them to see their favorite therapist—or they select as companions people who are. They develop a network of relationships in which people are absorbed for a significant portion of their waking hours in understanding their unconscious motivations, their interpersonal relationships, or their dreams. It is the members of this community who are most inclined to seek help anew from therapists each time their own problems, their relational difficulties, or their children's crises get out of hand. They are also the ones who take the therapeutic method home, employing it in working through tensions with intimates, reading about it in spare moments, and constantly using it to understand everyday life.

A community of enthusiasts evolves: the teachers, the practitioners, the consumers, the faithful, the curious, and the hangers-on. Within this community, therapy becomes the treatment of choice for a growing list of ailments, and for many people, almost a way of life. And of course, with the evolution of such a community, and the extension of therapeutic interventions into more aspects of modern life, there are significant shifts in the meaning of termination.

The Triumph of the Therapeutic

The concept of a community of therapy consumers is not new. It has been described by social theorists, notably Philip Rieff (1959, 1968) and Robert Bellah et al. (1985). They both begin with the premise that the psychologization of everyday life has proceeded further and faster than Freud ever imagined possible. It is not that people experience more intense personal difficulties than ever before, but that these difficulties are thought of and discussed in more psychological terms. The sensitivity groups and growth experiences of the sixties and seventies, along with the proliferation of therapies—Gestalt, transactional analysis, primal scream, family therapy, play therapy with children, and so on—have introduced a mass audience to Freud's invention. The record sales of pop-psychology books and the popularity of "trainings" in personal growth and of self-help groups are evidence of the venture's success.

According to Rieff, the therapeutic is taken up within a "negative community." A positive community is one that offers "some sort of salvation to the individual through participant membership" (Rieff, 1968, p. 71). Of old, the township or the church offered a positive sense of community. And until the modern age, it was the community that healed. The therapist—and Rieff here applies the term broadly to include the clergyman, the shaman, the physician, the sage, and the community leader—would comprehend the individual's difficulties in terms of alienation from the larger community and would heal the individual by integrating him or her back into the community and its symbol system.

All such efforts to reintegrate the subject into the communal symbol system may be categorized as "commitment therapies." Behind the shaman and priest, philosopher and physician, stands the great community as the ultimate corrective of personal disorders. Culture is the system of significances attached to behavior by which a society explains itself to itself. (1968, pp. 68–69)

Rieff believes that this kind of positive community no longer exists. It has broken into pieces and is no longer able to supply a coherent system of symbolic integration. There is no traditional community—though there are many vying subcommunities—that can offer salvation to the individual. In the vacuum, negative communities spring up. They do not offer a type of collective salvation, such as the church offers its members, but rather offer the individual a personal cure. The individual must rely on science and technology, on new forms of knowledge and expert types of personal cures, instead of hoping for reintegration into a larger positive community and its symbol system. The treatment, in line with the American emphasis on independence and individuality, must foster self-reliance and strength.

Freud's psychoanalytic psychotherapy fits the bill perfectly, and this explains its success in the modern age: "The assumption of the analytic theory is that there is no positive community standing behind the therapist. . . . The modern therapeutic idea is to empty those meanings that link the individual to dying worlds by assents of faith for which his analytic reason tells him he is not truly responsible" (Rieff, 1968, 76–77). For Rieff, the community of psychoanalysts, their patients, and their followers becomes the prototypic negative community of the modern age.

We now have available an interesting empirical study of the therapeutic negative community Rieff described. Robert Bellah et al. report on their five-year study of "the resources Americans have for making sense of their lives" (Bellah et al., 1985). They concentrate on the American middle class, which they believe has been "peculiarly central" and "dominant" in American society in this century. They divide their study into four separate research projects, one of which involves interviewing therapists, psychologists, and psychiatrists about modern life. (The others are interviews with middle-class couples about love and marriage, interviews with members of intact townships where citizens are still involved in public life, and interviews with members of socially concerned organizations.)

These researchers organize their data by speaking of various "lifestyle enclaves," somewhat akin to Rieff's negative communities. Individuals fit themselves into various lifestyle enclaves in order to find meaning in their lives. One of these enclaves is "the therapeutic culture." They write:

> Though the term "community" is widely and loosely used by Americans, and often in connection with lifstyle, we would like to reserve it for a more specific meaning. Whereas a community attempts to be an inclusive whole, celebrating the interdependence of public and private life and of the different callings of all, lifestyle is fundamentally segmental and celebrates the narcissism of similarity. It usually explicitly involves a contrast with others who "do not share one's lifestyle." For this reason, we speak not of lifestyle communities, though they are often called such in contemporary usage, but of lifestyle enclaves. Such enclaves are segmental in two senses. They involve only a segment of each individual, for they concern only private life, especially leisure and consumption. And they are segmental socially in that they include only those with a common lifestyle. The different, those with other lifestyles, are not necessarily despised. They may be willingly tolerated. But they are irrelevant or even invisible in terms of one's own lifestyle enclave. (p. 72)

In their portrayal of a therapist named Margaret Oldham, Bellah et al. present a picture of life in the therapeutic lifestyle enclave. Oldham, a therapist in her early thirties who lives and practices in a Southern community, is married to an engineer. She was raised by strict, hard-working, and very moral parents and is very proud of having done well in her studies. She attributes her sense of responsibility to her parents. She chose to be a therapist because she was curious about "what made people tick." She is very self-reliant, and makes this a central part of her definition of mental health:

> I do think it's important for you to take responsibility for your-
> self, I mean, nobody else is going to really do it. I mean peo-
> ple do take care of each other, people help each other, you
> know, when somebody's sick, and that's wonderful. In the end,
> you're really alone and you really have to answer to yourself,
> and in the end, if you don't get the job you want or, you
> know, meet the person you want, it's at least in part your
> responsibility. I mean your knight in shining armor is not going
> to meet you on the street and leave messages all over the
> world trying to find you. It's not going to happen. (p. 15)

Margaret Oldham likes her work: "Just the opportunity to get close to people in the way that you do in therapy is real nice and you grow a lot. You get better and better at sharing your emotions and giving to other people." But when her interviewer asks how therapy contributes to the larger social world, Margaret shakes her head and smiles ruefully: "The only community I ever think I'm adding to is the one of people who have been in therapy, and talk like psychologists, you know, and that's not particularly positive" (pp. 70–71).

Rieff and Bellah et al. share a concern that with the triumph of the therapeutic comes a certain moral impoverishment. They cite Alexis de Tocqueville's (1835) observation that the American version of democracy, based as it is on the self-made man's au- tonomy and seemingly infinite potential, will always be accom- panied by an extreme and ultimately harmful individualism. Ac- cording to de Tocqueville, individuals learn to feel that "they owe nothing to any man, they expect nothing from any man; they acquire the habit of always considering themselves as stand- ing alone, and they are apt to imagine that their whole destiny is in their own hands" (cited in Rieff, 1968, p. 70). Of course, the flip side of the self-made-man ideology is that, if individuals fail to attain wealth and happiness, they have no one to blame but themselves—and then a course of therapy to treat the inner foible behind the failure seems all the more logical.

Wayne

Wayne came to see me complaining of massive anxiety and insomnia that began about a month before, or just after he was named chairman of his department at a university.

I'm forty-three, I've always been very successful as an academic, and I've always insisted on staying away from a leadership role in campus politics. I like everybody to like me, and they do—for my teaching and writing. Stupidly, I let the others twist my arm into becoming chairman of the department. Now I can never sleep, I wake up at 5 a.m. worried about one issue or another, and I'm nervous all the time.

Wayne was preoccupied with concerns about the previous chairman who had been forced by his colleagues to resign, creating the opening Wayne filled. He did not need an interpretation from me to realize the link between his guilt about harming the previous chairman—an older man whose competence had for years been coming into question—and earlier conflicts about a father in whom he had been disappointed at an early age. After we discussed his guilt and his early history for a while, he concluded that his colleagues removed the previous chairman for cause, and Wayne's willingness to accept the position did not really affect the decision.

After eight sessions, Wayne reported the anxiety was under control and he was sleeping fine. It was at this point that he asked: "So I guess the question is do I need to continue therapy any longer?" As I discussed in chapter 6, Wayne is not alone in questioning the utility of continuing therapy after initial symptoms abate. I also explained how, today, with the majority of people undergoing therapy, not analysis, the ground rules are different. While analysands enter analysis with the intention of seeing it through to its natural termination years later, clients, even those in the core of the community, enter psychotherapy with more immediate goals and a much briefer time frame. And often, though they might drop out of therapy long before analysts would agree a "well-worked-through" termination could occur, they are also more likely to return to therapy at a later date when problems again overwhelm capacities to cope.

I think it is fair to say that Wayne, like Alan, demonstrates some clearly narcissistic traits. It is not only his conflicts involving relationships with men, rivalry, potency, and disappointment. He also tends to idealize me, and tells me so: "I feel really lucky to have found a therapist who's sharp enough to figure that out about me so quickly." But in the very next session he complains that eventually he would have figured out all the things I told him, and that my fee is really too high considering the area I work in, and that my office looks so little like a professional suite.

And Wayne presents other characteristic symptoms. He has no deep friendships except with his wife, and that relationship is in trouble. He feels she nags him, constantly demanding he be more emotionally present with her. They argue. He also feels empty, and uninvolved in his work activities. He spends his free time vigorously competing in the sports at which he excels, or doing fix-it projects around the house. He is very vulnerable to attack from others, for instance falling into a depression when a critical review of his book appears.

Even though I can demonstrate some narcissistic traits—perhaps the full-blown personality disorder—I do not believe it is fair for a therapist to imply to a high-functioning individual that, in the same way that hysterical paralysis *requires* therapy, so does the narcissistic personality. Rather, I try in one way or another to communicate to the client that the need for therapy is relative, and he has a choice in the matter. I responded to Wayne's question by saying: "That depends on what you want to get out of therapy. Your initial symptoms are gone, and so you've accomplished a lot. The question is whether or not you want to proceed and explore other aspects of your life—for instance, you've expressed concerns about your marriage."

It turns out in fact that Wayne had been referred to me by his wife, who had been in therapy with someone else for some time, and had resolved that she had a right to confront Wayne about his emotional aloofness and demand more from him. Wayne's wife, after years of passively accepting his inattention and his expectation that she perform wifely duties such as hosting his colleagues and taking care of their two children while he wrote his books, went to see a therapist complaining of depression. Her therapist helped her get in touch with ways she felt abused by Wayne and resentful. She slowly developed a network of friends who supported her demands, and she began to demand more from Wayne—about sharing housework as well as sharing feelings and psychological events. Now, his wife was essentially telling Wayne that as she became more psychologically sophisiticated and capable of using insight to improve the quality of her intimacies, he must change or risk losing her. Wayne's motivation to be in therapy thus stemmed not only from his work concerns—though these were the easier ones for him to name—but also from his fear that if he did not change, his wife would leave him.

Not infrequently a depressed woman will begin in therapy and begin to experience greater self-esteem. Her newfound discovery will release a previously repressed well of anger, and she will begin to demand more from a mate. The husband or lover is forced to decide whether to dig in and fight defensively to regain previous forms of power in the relationship, or to struggle with the woman and look into his part in the tensions that erupt in the relationship. In many instances, the man ultimately finds that the necessary changes are not so much a relinquishing of power to the woman as an opportunity to grow beyond prior personal limitations. Wayne was not sure which route he wanted to take when he began with me, and that is why he spoke only of his problems at work in our early sessions. Besides, it was clear he thought it unmanly to admit the real reason he had come to talk intimately with another man was his fear he might have trouble holding onto his wife. By the time we had discussed all these issues, it became clear that Wayne was motivated to continue in long-term, open-ended therapy and that eventually we would negotiate a termination date that each of us would feel was right.

In effect, Wayne's wife had entered the community of therapy consumers and was demanding that he do the same. It was his wife's demands that drove him into therapy, but it would be his choice about how far he wanted to enter the community of therapy consumers, and his choice about what would determine whether he remained in therapy after the symptoms disappeared. He was seriously considering following his wife's counsel (however much it sounded like an ultimatum), and undergoing therapy for the express purpose of communicating better with her, and being more at home with psychologically minded people. This seemed to me a rational choice. But if he had chosen not to continue in therapy, that would have seemed to me equally reasonable.

Thus the very existence of the community of therapy consumers affects the way termination is managed. Though therapists never discuss it in quite these terms, the decision to proceed in therapy, like the decision to alter some of the more troublesome aspects of one's character structure, is also a decision about how one wants to relate to that community, or to the people in that community (like Wayne's wife) whom one cares about.

Conclusion

PEOPLE OF different historical times and different social contexts complain of different symptoms. The symptoms reflect the times, as do the psychological theories that attempt to explain the symptoms. In fact, the whole concept of emotional symptomatology in sane people, as well as the idea of paying a specialist to listen and help with personal dilemmas, is a thoroughly modern invention.

Can we imagine a factory worker a century ago, or even a generation, after a long day at back-breaking labor for barely enough wages to feed his family, going to visit a therapist to complain of feeling empty or unspontaneous? And would inner foibles be seen as the root of his unhappiness? More likely a social phenomenon—for instance, the exploitation of workers—would be seen as the root of that worker's personal difficulty. Today we are less likely to attempt to explain modern alienation by examining the social arrangements, but are rather inclined to look within for a personal flaw that might account for our dissatisfactions.

As more people come to believe there is an inner flaw that explains their everyday unhappiness, the psychotherapy industry expands. More people seek the counsel of psychotherapists for more diverse problems than ever before. At the same time, there is a trend in the clinical literature toward the diagnosis of ever deeper-lying or more varied psychopathologies to justify ever more psychotherapy for just about anyone. This psychologization of everyday life is the context within which the meaning of termination must be understood.

I have contrasted two therapeutic modalities, long-term and

brief psychotherapy. And I have demonstrated that the social distribution of the two modalities not only is inequitable but also contradicts the clinical logic. The point is not that one or the other modality is preferable from a clinical or a social perspective. Each has its pros and cons. And it should be obvious from what I have presented of my clinical approach that I am not antitherapy. My own personal therapy has changed my life in large and wonderful ways. I practice and teach psychotherapy, brief and long-term, and like my work very much. I help people get past obstructions and grow. What could be more rewarding? I believe, in very many cases, psychotherapy can be of great benefit. And I believe, in some abstract way, that therapy contains much potential to foster social progress. For instance, because of therapy, a whole community of intimates and friends have become more open about feelings, more sensitive, more willing to be self-critical and to work through with each other the underlying issues in their occasional disputes. What if, on a social level, everyone were to change in this direction?

And I believe there is much that is useful in the clinical framework. Much can be learned from experienced clinicians and the rich tradition of psychoanalysis many of them bring to bear in their studies. In order to practice quality therapy, and to learn from the literature and the accumulated wisdom of therapists, the clinician must be well versed in psychopathology and the theory and technique of psychotherapy. The problem arises when the clinical logic becomes the exclusive consideration—as it so clearly has become in the professional training programs and literature.

In conclusion, I will return to a question Freud (1937) raised: Is psychotherapy terminable or interminable? It is my view that when the focus is narrowed to an exclusively clinical one, as it is for many therapists today, and much of what once was considered part of our common unhappiness is ascribed to psychopathology, psychotherapy becomes interminable.

In chapter 2 I cited Marion Milner's (1950) comment about the analyst's didactic personal analysis: "Perhaps we, as analysts, are handicapped in knowing all about what ending feels like, for by the mere fact of becoming analysts we have succeeded in bypassing an experience which our patients have to go through.

We have chosen to identify ourselves with our analyst's profession and to act out that identification" (p. 191).

Milner is here echoing Freud's (1937) concern about the interminability of psychoanalysis: "Every analyst should periodically—at intervals of five years or so—submit himself to analysis once more, without feeling ashamed of taking this step. This would mean, then, that not only the therapeutic analysis of patients but his own analysis would change from terminable into an interminable task" (p. 249). Of course, the candidate in the psychoanalytic institute has symptoms, and the training analysis has its therapeutic aspects. But because it is partly "didactic," and because it is a requirement for admission into the official group of analysts, there are differences. Freud was noting the difference when he commented that psychoanalysts should submit to repeat analyses. Milner's point is that the analyst never really leaves his own analyst. Rather, he merely assumes his role, joins his institute, and continues the analytic process with other analysands, perhaps younger candidates. In other words, there is a community of psychoanalysts that one can join, and if one does, then the meaning of one's own termination is changed.

Today, in the community of therapy consumers, as in Freud's inner circle, there is a tendency for therapy to become interminable. The community of therapy consumers includes many therapists, of course, but also many clients and ex-clients. This is the community of people who, like the analysts and their fellow-travelers, make "the therapeutic" a way of life. Since so many people undergo and practice a more delimited version of therapy today, this community is no longer limited to analysts and aristocratic or academic hangers-on. And in this community, just as in the community of analysts Milner referred to, termination is diffused to the extent that the participants live out the therapeutic. Rieff's concern becomes reality: "The successful patient has learned to withdraw from the painful tension of assent and dissent in his relations to society by relating himself more affirmatively to his depths. His newly acquired health entails a self-concern that takes precedence over social concerns and encourages an attitude of ironic insight on the part of the self toward all that is not self" (Rieff, 1959, p. 330).

Would Freud have approved of the extent of psychologization

we are witnessing today? It seems to me he was ambivalent about it, judging from some of his written statements, and then from the behavior of his inner circle. He wrote that psychoanalysis should be short-lived and was not needed by everyone: "Let us start from the assumption that what analysis achieves for neurotics is nothing other than what normal people accomplish for themselves without its help" (1937, p. 225). And he countered his concern about the interminability of analysis with statements like this:

> I am not intending to assert that analysis is altogether an endless business. . . . Every experienced analyst will be able to recall a number of cases in which he has bidden his patient a permanent farewell. . . . Our aim will not be to rub off every peculiarity of human character for the sake of a schematic "normality," nor yet to demand that the person who has been "thoroughly analyzed" shall feel no passions and develop no internal conflicts. The business of the analysis is to secure the best possible psychological conditions for the functions of the ego; with that it has discharged its task. (1937, pp. 249–50)

But as many times as Freud stated clearly he meant analysis only for certain symptoms and certain neurotics, he made some statement about the wider applicability of psychoanalysis—for example, to the understanding of psychosomatic ailments, criminality, creativity and political motivations. On the one hand, he wanted to guarantee that his method would never be applied wholesale by less than discriminating therapists; on the other, he wanted to guarantee the admission of psychoanalysis into every part of culture and everyday life so that its lessons would never be forgotten.

Still, there is some evidence that Freud did not believe that introspection, to the exclusion of social activity, was particularly healthy. He writes:

> Later, the ego learns that there is yet another way of securing satisfaction besides the *adaptation* to the external world which I have described. It is also possible to intervene in the external world by *changing* it, and to establish in it inten-

tionally the conditions which make satisfaction possible. This
activity then becomes the ego's highest function; decisions as
to when it is more expedient to control one's passions and bow
before reality, and when it is more expedient to side with them
and to take arms against the external world—such decisions
make up the whole essence of worldly wisdom. (1926, p. 201)

Whatever message he intended in his writings, his lived experience with colleagues, analysands, and followers did serve to
foster the kind of psychologization of everyday life we know today. In Freud's inner circle, practically everyone was at one time
in analysis with Freud, or later with one of Freud's analysands.
How can one speak of the termination of analysis when the analyst continues to have the last word in regard to theory, ex-
pulsion from the inner circle of those who dissent too vocifer-
ously, and consolidation of loyalty among the remaining followers?
Consider this interpretation of Jung's rebelliousness that Freud
shared with one of his loyal followers: "When Jung used his first
independent experiences to shake himself free of analysis, we
both knew that he had strong neurotic motives that took advantage of this discovery. I was then able to say with justification
that his twisted character did not compensate me for his lop-
sided theories" (Freud and Abraham, 1965, p. 352, cited in
Roustang, 1982, p. 7).

Freud's elite circle of pioneer analysts, their cohesion fostered
by the shared belief they needed to crusade to make the world
safe for psychoanalysis, engaged in clinical seminars, theoretical
debates, and mutual referral networks and collaborated on the
analysis of art, culture, history, and everyday life. According to
D. H. Lawrence (1921), they even started to look like their
founder: "A sinister look came into the eyes of the initiates—
the famous, or infamous, Freud look. You could recognize it
everywhere, wherever you went" (p. 3). The feeling among them
must have been that the psychoanalytic process is not only interminable, but also all-pervasive. They proceeded to apply it
to every aspect of everyday life.

Today's community of therapy consumers is heir to that original community of avid fans of psychoanalysis, Freud's inner circle. As among Freud and his colleagues, psychological explora-

tion becomes a way of life. An underlying assumption is that the quality of one's intimacies, the level of creativity, and one's feelings of inner emptiness are all symptoms amenable to therapeutic intervention. It is as if the client's capacity to join comfortably the community of therapy consumers, where intimacy, creativity, and meaning are the ideals, is the ultimate sign of mental health, and the signal that termination is properly near at hand. Therapy becomes a training in how to live the psychological life, or, better, how to live in that sophisticated community of the new elite: therapy-wise consumers. And there is always the possibility of undergoing more therapy whenever the need arises.

In effect, the members of this community share that internalized therapist, much as a clan shares a totem. As the therapist is internalized, so is a whole worldview. However neutral the particular therapist feels she or he is, she or he is spreading a very specific message about the proper conduct of lives. First, the therapist confirms there is a flaw deep within that explains one's feelings of alienation and also calls for a course of psychotherapy. Then the therapist, in conducting the therapy, presents the client with this prescription: Analyze actions and fantasies, search for meanings instead of acting out impulsively, try to be in touch with feelings, or, if the problem is a tendency to be overwhelmed by feelings, always remember to think things through and be confident there will be no falling apart. Whatever the particular words therapists tailor for specific clients, the therapist's maxim is always to give the inner life a place of priority in one's conscious ruminations. Wisdom does flow from this way of thinking, and for many the message is quite compelling.

This is a staunchly political message: as people become more absorbed in the psychological life, they become on the average less concerned about social dramas. After all, the same sensibility that drives one to seek ever deeper layers of truth in the psychological sphere might as easily drive one to seek an understanding of social tragedies and attempt to remedy them. The same quest for growth that drives one to change one's psychological makeup might as easily drive one to struggle to change the social arrangements. But because there seems to be no public forum to accomplish the latter kind of change, and little hope for real social progress, many people turn their attention inward where real gains seem possible. Even the 60s generation of rebels and radicals has fallen prey. Many are just as committed therapy consumers today as they were activists then. As people get used to consulting therapists for help addressing more of their everyday problems—including unhappiness at work, problems raising children, domestic violence—they become less practiced in social or collective solutions to these problems. And once we assume the unhappiness emanates entirely from a flaw deep within, we tend to seek more and better therapy whenever we experience more unhappiness. Clinicians are quick to devise new theories and new therapies. The endlessness of the quest explains the interminable nature of therapy.

References

Adler, G. (1986). Psychotherapy of the Narcissistic Personality Disorder Patient: Two Contrasting Approaches. *American Journal of Psychiatry*, 143:430–36.

Alexander, F. (1952). Development of the Fundamental Concepts of Psychoanalysis. In *Dynamic Psychiatry*, ed. F. Alexander and H. Ross. Chicago: University of Chicago Press, 3–34.

———, and T. French. (1946). *Psychoanalytic Therapy*. New York: Ronald Press.

Amada, G. (1983). The Interlude between Short- and Long-Term Psychotherapy. *American Journal of Psychotherapy*, 37:357–64.

American Psychiatric Association. (1980). *Diagnostic and Statistical Manual of Mental Disorders: DSM-III*. Washington, D.C.

———. (1987a). *Psychiatric News*, Jan. 2, 1987.

———. (1987b). *Revised Diagnostic and Statistical Manual of Mental Disorders: DSM-III-R*. Washington, D.C.

Andreas-Salomé, L. (1962). The Dual Orientation of Narcissism. *Psychoanalytic Quarterly*, 31:1–30.

Baker, H., and M. Baker. (1987). Heinz Kohut's Self Psychology: An Overview. *American Journal of Psychiatry*, 144:1–9.

Balint, M. (1950). On the Termination of Analysis. *International Journal of Psychoanalysis*, 31:196–99.

———. (1954). Analytische Ausbildung und Lehranalyse. *Psyche* (Stuttgart), 7:698–99.

Becker, E. (1973). *The Denial of Death*. New York: Free Press.

Bellah, R., R. Madson, W. Sullivan, A. Swidler, and S. Tipton. (1985). *Habits of the Heart: Individualism and Commitment in American Life*. Berkeley: University of California Press.

Bennett, M. (1983). Focal Psychotherapy—Terminable and Interminable. *American Journal of Psychotherapy*, 37:365–77.

Boyer, B., and P. Giovacchini. (1967, 1980). *Psychoanalytic Treatment of Schizophrenia, Borderline and Characterological Disorders*. New York: Jason Aronson.

Caplan, G. (1961). *An Approach to Community Mental Health.* New York: Grune and Stratton.

Chu, F., and S. Trotter. (1974). *The Madness Establishment.* New York: Grossman.

Clance, P., and S. Imes. (1978). The Impostor Phenomenon in High Achieving Women: Dynamics and Therapeutic Intervention. *Psychotherapy: Theory, Research and Practice,* 15:241–46.

Cooper, D. (1970). *The Death of the Family.* New York: Vintage.

Davanloo, H., ed. (1978). *Basic Principles and Techniques in Short-Term Dynamic Psychotherapy.* London: Spectrum.

Deutsch, H. (1942). Some Forms of Emotional Disturbance and Their Relationship to Schizophrenia. *Psychoanalytic Quarterly,* 11:301–21.

Dewald, P. (1964). *Psychotherapy: A Dynamic Approach.* New York: Basic Books.

Ekstein, R. (1965). Working Through and Termination of Analysis. *Journal of the American Psychoanalytic Association,* 13:57–78.

Fairbairn, W. R. D. (1941). A Revised Psychopathology of the Psychoses and Psychoneuroses. In *Psychoanalytic Studies of the Personality.* London: Tavistock, 1952, 28–58.

Fenichel, O. (1924). From the Terminal Phase of Analysis. In *Collected Papers.* New York: Norton, 1953, 1:27–31.

Ferenczi, S. (1927). The Problem of the Termination of the Analysis. In *The Selected Papers of Sandor Ferenczi: Problems and Methods of Psychoanalysis,* ed. M. Balint. New York: Basic Books, 1955, 3:77–86.

——, and O. Rank. (1925). *The Development of Psychoanalysis.* Trans. C. Newton. New York: Nervous and Mental Disease Publishing.

Firestein, S. K. (1978). *Termination in Psychoanalysis.* New York: International Universities Press.

Forward, S., and J. Torres. (1986). *Men Who Hate Women and the Women Who Love Them.* New York: Bantam.

Freud, S. (1900). *The Interpretation of Dreams. Standard Edition,* 4:1–630. London: Hogarth, 1957–61.

——. (1905a). *Fragment of an Analysis of a Case of Hysteria. Standard Edition,* 7:3–124. London: Hogarth, 1957–61.

——. (1905b). *Three Essays on the Theory of Sexuality. Standard Edition,* 7:125–248. London: Hogarth, 1957–61.

——. (1910). *Five Lectures. Standard Edition,* 11:3–58. London: Hogarth, 1957–61.

——. (1912). The Dynamics of the Transference. *Standard Edition,* 12:97–108. London: Hogarth, 1957–61.

—— (1913). Further Recommendations on the Technique of Psychoanalysis: On Beginning the Treatment. *Standard Edition,* 12:121–44. London: Hogarth, 1957–61.

——. (1914). Recollecting, Repeating and Working Through. *Standard Edition,* 12:146–56. London: Hogarth, 1957–61.

——. (1915). The Unconscious. *Standard Edition,* 14:159–218.

——. (1918). *From the History of an Infantile Neurosis. Standard Edition*, 17:3–124. London: Hogarth, 1957–61.

——. (1920). *Beyond the Pleasure Principle. Standard Edition*, 18:3–66. London: Hogarth, 1957–61.

——. (1926a). *Inhibitions, Symptoms and Anxiety. Standard Edition*, 20:77–178. London: Hogarth, 1957–61.

——. (1926b). *The Question of Lay Analysis. Standard Edition*, 20:179–260. London: Hogarth, 1957–61.

——. (1937). Analysis Terminable and Interminable. *Standard Edition*, 23:209–54. London: Hogarth, 1957–61.

——, and K. Abraham. (1965). *A Psychoanalytic Dialogue: The Letters of S. Freud and K. Abraham 1907–1926.* Ed. H. Abraham and E. Freud. New York: Basic Books.

——, and J. Breuer. (1895). *Studies on Hysteria. Standard Edition*, 2:1–309. London: Hogarth Press, 1957–61

Fromm-Reichmann, F. (1950). *Principles of Intensive Psychotherapy.* Chicago: University of Chicago Press.

Gaskill, H. (1980). The Closing Phase of the Psychoanalytic Treatment of Adults and the Goals of Psychoanalysis: The Myth of Perfectability. *International Journal of Psychoanalysis*, 61:11–23.

Gill, M. (1954). Psychoanalysis and Exploratory Psychotherapy. *Journal of the American Psychoanalytic Association*, 2:771–97.

——, and H. Muslin. (1978). Transference in the Dora Case. *Journal of the American Psychoanalytic Association*, 26:311–31.

Glover, E. (1955). *The Technique of Psychoanalysis.* New York: International Universities Press.

Goldberg, A. (1973). Psychotherapy of Narcissistic injuries. *Archives of General Psychiatry*, 28:722–26.

Green, A. (1975). The Analyst, Symbolization and Absence in the Analytic Setting (On Changes in Analytic Practice and Analytic Experience). *International Journal of Psychoanalysis*, 56:1–22.

Greenson, R. (1966). Discussion. In *Psychoanalysis in the Americas*, ed. R. Litman. New York: International Universities Press, 263–66.

——. (1967). *The Technique and Practice of Psychoanalysis.* New York: International Universities Press.

Greenspan, M., and N. Kulish. (1985). Factors in Termination in Long-Term Psychotherapy. *Psychotherapy*, 22:75–82.

Grotstein, J. (1981). *Splitting and Projective Identification.* New York: Jason Aronson.

Guntrip, H. (1975). My Experience of Analyses with Fairbairn and Winnicott. *International Review of Psychoanalysis*, 2:145–56. In *Psychoanalytic Practice.* New York: Grune and Stratton, 1977, 49–67.

Gustafson, J. (1983). Winnicott and Sullivan in the Brief Psychotherapy Clinic, Parts 1–3. *Contemporary Psychoanalysis*, 19:624–672.

——. (1986). *The Complex Secret of Brief Psychotherapy.* New York: Norton.

Held, R. (1955). Les Critères de la fin du traitement psychanalytique. *Revue Français de la Psychanalyse*, 19:603–14.

Holden, M. (1983). *The Use of the Negative Transference in a Follow-Up Session: Its Impact on Short-Term Psychotherapy*. Diss. Berkeley: Wright Institute.

Horowitz, M. (1976). *Stress Response Syndromes*. New York: Jason Aronson.

——, C. Marmer, J. Krupnick, et al. (1984). *Personality Styles and Brief Psychotherapy*. New York: Jason Aronson.

Jacoby, R. (1983). *The Repression of Psychoanalysis: Otto Fenichel and the Political Freudians*. London: Harper and Row.

Jacques, E. (1965). Death and the Midlife Crisis. *International Journal of Psychoanalysis*, 46:502–14.

Jones, E. (1953–55). *The Life and Work of Sigmund Freud*. 2 vols. New York: Basic Books.

Kardiner, A. (1977). *My Analysis with Freud: Reminiscences*. New York: Norton.

Kernberg, O. (1975). *Borderline Conditions and Pathological Narcissism*. New York: Jason Aronson.

——. (1984). *Severe Personality Disorders: Psychotherapeutic Strategies*. New Haven: Yale University Press.

Khan, M. (1963). Silence as a Communication. *Bulletin of the Menninger Clinic*, 21:300–13.

Klein, M. (1948). *Contributions to Psycho-Analysis: 1921–1945*. London: Hogarth.

——. (1950). On the Criteria for the Termination of a Psycho-Analysis. *International Journal of Psychoanalysis*, 31:78–80.

Kohut, H. (1971). *The Analysis of the Self: A Systematic Approach to the Psychoanalytic Treatment of Narcissistic Personality Disorders*. New York: International Universities Press.

——. (1977). *The Restoration of the Self*. New York: International Universities Press.

——. (1979). The Two Analyses of Mr. Z. *International Journal of Psychoanalysis*, 60:3–27.

——, and E. Wolf. (1978). The Disorders of the Self and Their Treatment: An Outline. *International Journal of Psychoanalysis*, 59:413–25.

Kris, A. (1982). *Free Association: Method and Process*. New Haven: Yale University Press.

Kuhn, T. (1962). *The Structure of Scientific Revolutions*. Chicago: University of Chicago Press.

Kupers, T. (1981). *Public Therapy: The Practice of Psychotherapy in the Public Mental Health Clinic*. New York: Free Press.

——. (1986). The Dual Potential of Brief Psychotherapy. *Free Associations*, 6:80–99.

Langs, R. (1973, 1974). *The Technique of Psychoanalytic Psychotherapy*. 2 Vols. New York: Jason Aronson.

Laplanche, J., and J.-B. Pontalis. (1973). *The Language of Psychoanalysis.* New York: Norton.

Lawrence, D. (1921). *Psychoanalysis and the Unconscious and Fantasia of the Unconscious.* New York: Viking, 1960.

Lichtman, R. (1982). *The Production of Desire.* New York: Free Press.

Lifschutz, J. (1984). What Is "Psychotherapy?" *International Journal of Psychoanalytic Psychotherapy,* 10:91–107.

Lipton, S. (1961). The Last Hour. *Journal of the American Psychoanalytic Association,* 9:325–30.

Loewald, H. (1960). On the Therapeutic Action of Psychoanalysis. *International Journal of Psychoanalysis,* 41:16–33.

Mack Brunswick, R. (1928). A Supplement to Freud's "History of an Infantile Neurosis." *International Journal of Psychoanalysis,* 9:439–476. In *The Wolfman,* 1971, 263–307.

Mahler, M. (1972). *Rapprochement Subphase of the Separation-Individuation Process. Selected Papers of Margaret S. Mahler,* 2 Vols. New York: Jason Aronson, 1979, 2:131–48.

Malan, D. (1973). Verbal Communication, Seminar on Brief Therapy, Tavistock Inst., London.

———. (1976). *The Frontier of Brief Psychotherapy.* London: Plenum.

———. (1979). *Individual Psychotherapy and the Science of Psychodynamics.* Boston: Butterworth.

Malcolm, J. (1981). *Psychoanalysis: The Impossible Profession.* New York: Knopf.

Mann, J. (1973). *Time-Limited Psychotherapy.* Cambridge: Harvard University Press.

Marmor, J. (1979). Short-Term Dynamic Psychotherapy. *American Journal of Psychiatry,* 136:149–55.

Martin, E., and R. Schurtman. (1985). Termination Anxiety as It Affects the Therapist. *Psychotherapy,* 22:92–96.

Masterson, J. (1976). *Psychotherapy of the Borderline Adult: A Developmental Approach.* New York: Brunner/Mazel.

Miller, A. (1981). *Prisoners of Childhood.* New York: Harper and Row.

Milner, M. (1950). A Note on the Ending of an Analysis. *International Journal of Psychoanalysis,* 31:191–93.

Nemetz, S. (reporter). (1979). Panel: Conceptualizing the Nature of the Therapeutic Action of Psychoanalytic Psychotherapy. *Journal of the American Psychoanalytic Association,* 27:127–44.

Ornstein, P. H. (1974). A Discussion of the Paper by Otto Kernberg on "Further Contributions to the Treatment of Narcissistic Personalities." *International Journal of Psychoanalysis,* 55:241–47.

Patterson, V., H. Levene, and L. Breger. (1977). A One-Year Follow-Up of Two Forms of Brief Psychotherapy. *American Journal of Psychotherapy,* 31:76.

Pumpian-Mindlin, E. (1958). Comments on Technique of Termination and

Transfer in a Clinic Setting. *American Journal of Psychotherapy*, 12:455.

Ramas, M. (1980). Freud's Dora, Dora's Hysteria: The Negation of a Woman's Rebellion. *Feminist Studies*, 6:471–510.

Rangell, L. (1966). An Overview of the Ending of an Analysis. In *Psychoanalysis in the Americas*, ed. R. Litman. New York: International Universities Press, 141–65.

Rank, O. (1924). *The Trauma of Birth*. London: Kegan Paul, 1929.

Reich, A. (1950). On the Termination of Analysis. *International Journal of Psychoanalysis*, 31:179–83. Also in *Psychoanalytic Contributions*. New York: International Universities Press, 1975, 121–35.

Reich, W. (1933). *Character Analysis*. New York: Farrar, Strauss and Giroux, 1972.

———. (1967). *Reich Speaks of Freud*. Ed. M. Higgins and C. Higgins. New York: Farrar, Straus and Giroux.

Rickman, J. (1950). On the Criteria for the Termination of an Analysis. In *Selected Contributions to Psychoanalysis*. New York: Basic Books, 1957, 127–30.

Rieff, P. (1959). *Freud: The Mind of a Moralist*. New York: Viking.

———. (1968). *The Triumph of the Therapeutic: Uses of Faith after Freud*. New York: Harper and Row.

Robinson, P. (1969). *The Freudian Left: Wilhelm Reich, Geza Roheim, Herbert Marcuse*. New York: Harper and Row.

Roustang, F. (1982). *Dire Mastery*. Baltimore: Johns Hopkins University Press.

Saul, L. (1958). Progression and Termination of the Analysis. In *Technique and Practice of Psychoanalysis*. Philadelphia: Lippincott, 224–31.

Schafer, R. (1973). The Termination of Brief Psychoanalytic Psychotherapy. *International Journal of Psychoanalytic Psychotherapy*, 2:135–48.

Schmideberg, M. (1938). After the Analysis. *Psychoanalytic Quarterly*, 7:122–42.

Sifneos, P. (1972). *Short-Term Psychotherapy and Emotional Crisis*. Cambridge: Harvard University Press.

———. (1973). The Prevalence of "Alexithymic" Characteristics in Psychosomatic Patients. *Psychotherapy and Psychosomatics*, 22:255–62.

Stone, L. (1954). The Widening Scope of Indications for Psychoanalysis. *Journal of the American Psychoanalytic Association*, 2:567–94.

———. (1961). *The Psychoanalytic Situation*. New York: International Universities Press.

Strachey, J. (1934). The Nature of the Therapeutic Action of Psychoanalysis. *International Journal of Psychoanalysis*, 15:127–59.

TenHouten, W., K. Hoppe, J. Bogen, and D. Walter. (1986). Alexithymia: An Experimental Study of Cerebral Commissurotomy Patients and Normal Control Subjects. *American Journal of Psychiatry*, 143:312–16.

Ticho, E. (1966). Discussion. In *Psychoanalysis in the Americas*, ed. R. Litman. New York: International Universities Press, 171–73.

———. (1970). Differences between Psychoanalysis and Psychotherapy. *Bulletin of the Menninger Clinic*, 34:128–38.

———. (1972). Termination of Psychoanalysis: Treatment Goals, Life Goals. *Psychoanalytic Quarterly*, 41:315–33.

Tocqueville, A. de. (1835, 1840) *Democracy in America*. Trans. G. Lawrence. Ed. J. P. Mayer. New York: Doubleday, Anchor, 1969.

Wallerstein, R. (1969). Introduction to Panel on Psychoanalysis and Psychotherapy. *International Journal of Psychoanalysis*, 50:117–28.

Weddington, W., and J. Cavenar. (1979). Termination Initiated by the Therapist: A Countertransference Storm. *American Journal of Psychiatry*, 136:1302–05.

Weigert, E. (1952). Contribution to the Problem of Terminating Psychoanalysis. In *The Courage to Love*. New Haven: Yale University Press, 1970, 249–63.

———. (1955). Special Problems in Connection with Termination of Training Analyses. In *The Courage to Love*. New Haven: Yale University Press, 1970, 264–75.

Winnicott, D. W. (1965). *The Family and Individual Development*. London: Tavistock.

———. (1971a). *Playing and Reality*. New York: Basic Books.

———. (1971b). *Therapeutic Consultations in Child Psychiatry*. New York: Basic Books.

Wolf, E. (1983). Empathy and Countertransference. In *The Future of Psychoanalysis*, ed. A. Goldberg. New York: International Universities Press, 309–26.

Wolfman. (1971). The Wolfman. Ed. M. Gardiner. New York: Basic Books.

Wortis, J. (1954). *Fragment of an Analysis with Freud*. New York: Simon and Schuster.

Index

DATE DUE

MAR 0 9 1993			
MAR 2 9 ENT'D SW MAR 2 6 1999			
SW/R APR 0 1 1999			